W9-AEK-903

Walch Hands-on Science Series

Atmosphere and Weather

by Karen Kwitter, Ph.D., and Steven Souza, Ph.D.

illustrated by
Lloyd Birmingham

J. WESTON

WALCH

PUBLISHER

Portland, Maine

User's Guide
to
Walch Reproducible Books

As part of our general effort to provide educational materials which are as practical and economical as possible, we have designated this publication a "reproducible book." The designation means that purchase of the book includes purchase of the right to limited reproduction of all pages on which this symbol appears:

Here is the basic Walch policy: We grant to individual purchasers of this book the right to make sufficient copies of reproducible pages for use by all students of a single teacher. This permission is limited to a single teacher, and does not apply to entire schools or school systems, so institutions purchasing the book should pass the permission on to a single teacher. Copying of the book or its parts for resale is prohibited.

Any questions regarding this policy or requests to purchase further reproduction rights should be addressed to:

Permissions Editor
J. Weston Walch, Publisher
321 Valley Street • P. O. Box 658
Portland, Maine 04104-0658

1   2   3   4   5   6   7   8   9   10
ISBN 0-8251-3764-0

⚡ Contents

Acknowledgment

The authors are grateful for the love and support of their parents: Arthur and Sonia Kwitter, and Manuel and Barbara Souza.

The authors thank their sons Randy and Aaron for their encouragement and for trying out some of these activities.

 # To the Teacher

This is one of a series of hands-on science activity books for middle school and early high school students. A recent national survey of middle school students conducted by the National Science Foundation (NSF) found that:

- more than half listed science as their favorite subject.
- more than half wanted more hands-on activities.
- 90 percent stated that the best way for them to learn science was to perform experiments themselves.

The books in this series seek to capitalize on these findings. These books are not texts but supplements. They offer hands-on, fun activities that will turn some students on to science. All of these activities can be done in school, and most of them can be done at home. The authors are teachers and have field-tested the activities in a public middle school and/or high school.

Students will need only basic equipment to carry out the experiments in this book. The activities range from the very simple to the difficult. There is something for every student.

THE ACTIVITIES CAN BE USED:

- to provide hands-on experiences relating to textbook content.
- to give verbally limited students a chance to succeed and gain extra credit.
- as the basis for class or school science fair projects or for other science competitions.
- to involve students in science club projects.
- as homework assignments.
- to involve parents in their children's science education and experiences.

Students can learn important scientific principles from carrying out these activities. For example:

- Negative experimental results are just as important as positive experimental results.
- Data may vary from what is expected.

Each activity has a Teacher Resource section that includes, besides helpful hints and suggestions, a scoring rubric, Internet connections for students who wish to carry out the follow-up activities, and a quiz. Instructional objectives and the National Science Standards that apply to each activity are provided to help you meet state and local expectations.

The State We're In: Air Is a Gas!

 INSTRUCTIONAL OBJECTIVES

Students will be able to

- describe the gaslike properties of air.
- demonstrate that air is compressible.
- record data in a table.
- draw conclusions based on data.

 NATIONAL SCIENCE STANDARDS ADDRESSED

Students demonstrate an understanding of

- the structure and properties of matter.
- relevant concepts to explain observed phenomena.
- analysis of data using mathematical concepts such as the mean.

Students demonstrate scientific inquiry and problem-solving skills by

- framing questions.
- working in teams to collect and share information and ideas.
- using technology and tools to observe and measure objects.

Students demonstrate effective scientific communication by

- arguing from evidence and data.

 MATERIALS

- Basketball or soccer ball
- Bicycle pump with needle adapter
- Triple-beam balance
- Tape measure

 = Safety icon

 INTERNET TIE-IN   http://dionysus.phs.uiuc.edu/~pearman/101Online/notes/gasses/gasses.html

HELPFUL HINTS AND DISCUSSION

Time frame: 40 minutes, or one class period
Structure: Groups of two or three students
Location: In class

In this activity, demonstrate that air has mass and exerts pressure on its container. Demonstrate the use of a triple-beam balance prior to the exercise. Review the meaning of the term *mean* and other mathematical concepts such as π and determining the volume of a sphere. Give definitions of density, diameter, and circumference.

SCORING RUBRIC

Full credit should be given to students who fill in the data tables appropriately and who answer the Concluding Questions correctly and in complete sentences. Extra credit can be given to students who do the Extension or Follow-Up activities. The quiz can be scored from 1 to 3 correct.

ADAPTATIONS FOR HIGH AND LOW ACHIEVERS

High Achievers: High achievers should be encouraged to do the Extension and Follow-Up activities.

Low Achievers: Prior to the experiment, review the material, particularly the mathematical concept that the difference between two measurements indicates a change. Also review the concept of density.

QUIZ
1. Which, if any, of the following four statements are true?
   a) Gases have no mass.
   b) Gases can be compressed.
   c) Air is not a gas.
   d) A fully inflated basketball weighs more than a partially inflated basketball.
2. Describe the variation in density as a typical substance changes from a solid to a liquid to a gas.
3. What happens to the density of air as it is compressed?

Name _____   Date _____

The State We're In: Air Is a Gas!

 BEFORE YOU BEGIN

Under ordinary conditions, like those in your classroom, matter can exist in one of three physical states: **solid**, **liquid**, or **gas**. Gases (and liquids) are fluids that flow and fill whatever container they are confined in. Although gases are generally much less dense than either liquids or solids, a volume of gas does have a measurable mass. Gases are also **compressible**. This means a given amount of a gas can be forced to occupy a smaller volume, or more gas can be added to a fixed volume. Compressing a gas increases the pressure it exerts on its container. Heating a gas reduces its density, therefore increasing its volume and/or pressure. Cooling a gas does the opposite. In this activity, you will investigate the gas we live in: air.

 MATERIALS

- Basketball or soccer ball
- Bicycle pump with needle adapter
- Triple-beam balance
- Tape measure

 = Safety icon

 PROCEDURE

1. Partly deflate the ball by inserting the needle adapter and squeezing until the ball partly collapses and loses its spherical shape. Using the pump and needle adapter, reinflate the ball until it just barely regains and holds its spherical shape. If you think you may have gone past this point, let some air out and try again. You can now assume that the ball is filled with air at the same atmospheric pressure as the air in your classroom.

2. Use the triple-beam balance to determine the mass of the just-barely-filled ball (case A). Write down the weight in kilograms in Table 1. Make your measurement as precise as possible. Have each team member repeat this procedure.

3. Next, measure the circumference of the ball with the tape measure. Record the value in meters in Table 2. Divide the circumference by π (= 3.14) to calculate the diameter of the ball, and record this value in Table 2. Have each member of your team repeat this procedure.

4. Compute and record in Tables 1 and 2 the average measured mass, circumference, and diameter for your team. (To calculate the average, add up the individual values and then divide by the number of observations being averaged.)

5. Now inflate the ball fully so that it bounces well enough to use in a game (case B). Repeat steps 2 to 4 for the fully inflated ball. **Do not overinflate the ball—it could explode and cause injury.**

6. Let enough air out of the fully inflated ball so that it's about half full. It is not important to be exact. Just be sure that the ball is less than fully inflated and more inflated than the just-barely-full ball. Repeat steps 2 to 4 for the half-full ball (case C).

7. Calculate the difference between the average mass of the fully inflated ball (case B) and that of the just-barely-filled ball (case A). Enter the value in Table 1 as the change in mass of the fully inflated ball (case B) relative to the just-barely-filled ball (case A). Next, calculate the difference

(continued)

The State We're In: Air Is a Gas! *(continued)*

between the average diameter of the fully inflated ball (case B) and that of the just-barely-filled ball (case A). Enter the value in Table 2 as the change in diameter of the fully inflated ball (case B) relative to the just-barely-filled ball (case A).

8. Repeat step 7 for the half-full ball (case C) relative to the just-barely-filled ball (case A).

EXTENSION Find the approximate density of the air in the fully inflated ball. The density is equal to the mass of air in the fully inflated ball divided by its volume. Calculate the volume of the ball in m^3 using this equation: Volume of a sphere = $\frac{4}{3}\pi r$. $R = D/2$. For D, use the average diameter listed in Table 2 under case B.

To calculate the density, you need to divide the mass of the air in the fully inflated ball (case B) by the volume that you just calculated. But, you don't know the mass of just the air in the fully inflated ball. Here's how to get around this problem: You do know that the air in the just-barely-inflated ball (case A) is at atmospheric pressure. Air at atmospheric pressure has a density of 1.29 kg/m^3. The volumes of the just-barely-inflated ball and the fully inflated ball are roughly the same. So, by multiplying the density of air at atmospheric pressure by that volume, you can find the mass of air in the just-barely-inflated ball (case A). Enter this value where indicated under Data Collection and Analysis. Add this mass to the difference in mass between the just-barely-full (case A) and fully inflated ball (case B) from Table 1. This sum represents the mass of the air in the fully inflated ball (case B). Enter this sum where indicated under Data Collection and Analysis. Divide this total mass by the volume of the ball, and you have calculated the density of the air in the fully inflated ball. Enter this value where indicated under Data Collection and Analysis. How many times more dense is the air in the fully inflated ball than air at atmospheric pressure?

DATA COLLECTION AND ANALYSIS

Table 1   **Mass of the Ball in Kilograms**

	case A (just barely filled)	case B (fully inflated)	case C (half full)
Student 1			
Student 2			
Student 3			
Average			
change in mass relative to case A	no change		

(continued)

The State We're In: Air Is a Gas! *(continued)*

Table 2   Circumference and Diameter of the Ball in Meters

	case A (just barely filled)	case B (fully inflated)	case C (half full)
Student 1 circumference: diameter:			
Student 2 circumference: diameter:			
Student 3 circumference: diameter:			
Average circumference: diameter:			
change in diameter relative to case A	no change		

EXTENSION

Volume of fully inflated ball: _____ m^3 Mass of air in just-barely-inflated ball: _____ kg

Mass of air in fully inflated ball: _____ kg   Density of air in fully inflated ball: _____ kg/m^3

CONCLUDING QUESTIONS

1. What happens to the mass of the ball as you inflate it and deflate it? Why? _____

    _____

    _____

    _____

    _____

2. Does the diameter of the ball change significantly (say, more than 20 percent) in its three states of inflation? Does this mean that air is compressible? Why or why not?

    _____

    _____

    _____

    _____

(continued)

The State We're In: Air Is a Gas! (continued)

3. Does air exhibit the properties of a solid, liquid, or gas? Explain how you draw this conclusion from your observations.

_____

_____

_____

_____

4. Did everyone in your group measure exactly the same masses and diameters in steps 2, 5, and 8? If not, what might be some reasons for this?

_____

_____

_____

_____

 Follow-up Activities

1. List some everyday objects that contain air at greater than atmospheric pressure.

2. Take two small party balloons, blow them up as equally as you can to a size of about 10 cm, and tie off their ends. Leave the first balloon at room temperature. Put the second in a freezer for 20 minutes. Remove it from the freezer and immediately compare its size with the room-temperature balloon. (It will warm up quickly!)

(continued)

The Chemical Composition of Air

 INSTRUCTIONAL OBJECTIVES

Students will be able to

- demonstrate that oxygen is a component of air.
- describe how oxidation produces rust.
- draw conclusions based on data.

 NATIONAL SCIENCE STANDARDS ADDRESSED

Students demonstrate an understanding of

- chemical reactions and conservation of matter.
- relevant concepts to explain observed phenomena.

Students demonstrate scientific inquiry and problem-solving skills by

- framing questions and identifying variables.
- working in teams to collect and share information and ideas.
- using technology and tools to observe and measure objects.

Students demonstrate effective scientific communication by

- arguing from evidence and data.
- representing data in multiple ways (Extension).

 MATERIALS

- Small, clear juice glass (preferably with straight sides)
- Steel wool pad (preferably without soap)
- $\frac{1}{2}$ cup white vinegar
- Toothpick
- Clear bowl, dish, or measuring cup wider and taller than the juice glass
- Plastic ruler with millimeter divisions

For the Extension:
- Graph paper or a computer graphing program

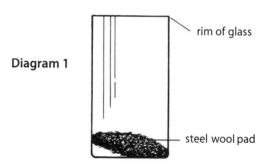

Diagram 1

rim of glass

steel wool pad

HELPFUL HINTS AND DISCUSSION

Time frame:	50 minutes, or one class period, plus 10 minutes the next day
Structure:	Groups of two or three students
Location:	In class

If the steel wool pads come with soap, the students should squeeze the pads under warm running water until the soap is gone. At the beginning of the experiment, the students pour vinegar over the pad to make sure that the steel wool surface is clean. It will be helpful if the glasses provided to the students have straight sides so that the relative volume occupied by the water can be estimated by measuring the water level. Instruct the students to make sure that the steel wool stays securely in the bottom of the glass when inverted, but also to avoid packing it tightly. Air in the glass should be able to reach all parts of the steel wool. It may be helpful to have the students practice steps 4 and 5 without water and vinegar, and step 6 with just the bowl, water, juice glass, and ruler.

ADAPTATIONS FOR HIGH AND LOW ACHIEVERS

High Achievers: High achievers should be encouraged to do the Extension and Follow-up activities.

Low Achievers: Review the material prior to the experiment. Also review the concepts of mixtures and fractional volumes.

SCORING RUBRIC

Full credit should be given to students who correctly fill in the data table and answer the questions in complete sentences. If the experiment fails to consume at least 10 percent of the air in the glass, the student should provide credible reasons in Concluding Question 2 to receive full credit. Extra credit should be given to students who complete the Extension or Follow-up activities. The quiz can be scored from 1 to 4 correct.

INTERNET TIE-INS   http://www.met.fsu.edu/explores/atmcomp.html
                        http://daac.gsfc.nasa.gov/CAMPAIGN_DOCS/ATM_CHEM/present_atmosphere.html
                        http://www.met.tamu.edu/class/Metr304/Exer2dir/exercise2.html

 QUIZ   1. What is the most chemically active component of air?
              2. What percentage of air molecules, by volume, is nitrogen?
              3. The process of burning coal, which chemically combines carbon with oxygen, is an
                 example of what chemical process?
              4. Does a given amount of oxygen in rust occupy much *less* or much *more* volume than
                 it did when it was in gaseous form in the atmosphere?

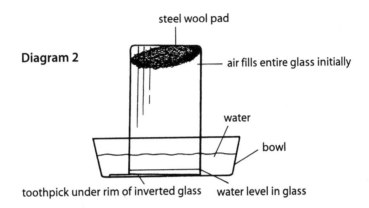

Name _____   Date _____

The Chemical Composition of Air

  BEFORE YOU BEGIN

Dry air is a mixture of gases. This mixture is composed primarily of nitrogen (N_2, 78% by volume), oxygen (O_2, 21%), and argon (Ar, 1%), with trace amounts of other gases. The amounts of these gases do not change appreciably with time or location, though other gases may be present in varying amounts. Although it is the most abundant atmospheric gas, nitrogen is not easy to detect directly because it is chemically not very active. However, oxygen is very active. It shows its presence in many ways—primarily by combining with other elements by a process called **oxidation**, to make compounds called **oxides**. Combustion (fire), rusting, and animal metabolism are all examples of oxidation.

In this activity, you will demonstrate the presence of oxygen in the atmosphere and estimate how much oxygen the atmosphere contains. Steps 1 through 6 must be done quickly, so you should first practice steps 4 and 5 without the water and vinegar.

 MATERIALS

- Small, clear juice glass (preferably with straight sides)
- Steel wool pad (preferably without soap)
- $\frac{1}{2}$ cup white vinegar
- Toothpick

- Clear bowl, dish, or measuring cup wider and taller than the juice glass
- Plastic ruler with millimeter divisions

For the Extension:
- Graph paper or a computer graphing program

 PROCEDURE

1. If the steel wool pad contains soap, hold it under warm running water and squeeze it until all of the soap is removed. Be thorough! If the pad does not contain soap, go to step 2.

2. Fill the bowl with water to a level of about 3 centimeters.

3. Soak the steel wool pad in vinegar for about 10 seconds. This will ensure that the steel wool surfaces are clean and that iron from the steel is exposed to air. Squeeze and shake out any excess vinegar.

4. Immediately after cleaning with vinegar, stuff the pad into the bottom of the juice glass. Make sure that it is secure enough to stay in place when the glass is turned upside down, but do not pack it tightly. Air should be able to circulate around the suspended pad. Best results are obtained if the pad is tilted as shown and held in place by contact with the sides of the glass. (See Diagram 1.)

Diagram 1

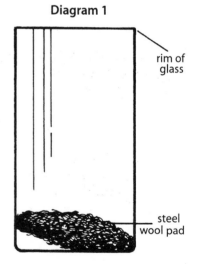

rim of glass

steel wool pad

5. Invert the glass, and holding it straight up-and-down, place it in the bowl filled with water, trapping air in the glass. Position the toothpick so that it sticks under the rim of the inverted glass. This will allow water to enter the glass from the bowl. (See Diagram 2.)   *(continued)*

The Chemical Composition of Air (continued)

6. Hold the ruler against the inverted glass and measure the height of the water in the glass (*not* in the bowl) to the nearest millimeter. Record this in the data table as the entry for Time = 0.

Oxygen molecules from the air inside the glass will react with the iron in the steel wool to form iron oxide, or rust, which is a solid. These oxygen molecules are then no longer part of the air. There are fewer air molecules inside the glass, which lowers the gas pressure there. This allows the water in the bowl, which is under normal atmospheric pressure, to enter the glass, raising the water level.

Diagram 2

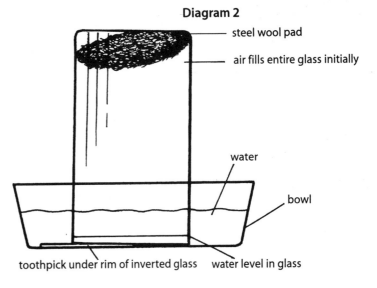

7. Measure the height of the column of water in the glass every 10 minutes for 30 minutes. Record measurements in the table. Also, record any changes in the appearance of the steel wool pad. The next day at about the same time of day, make a final measurement of the height of the water in the glass and record it.

8. Measure the total height of the glass (T) and enter it where indicated. You can now estimate the fraction of the volume of the glass that is occupied by water. For a glass with straight sides, this will be the same as the fraction of the glass's total height that is filled with water, which is just the measured height of the water divided by T. For each measured height, calculate and enter this value under Fractional Volume. Express your results as two-place decimal fractions.

 DATA COLLECTION AND ANALYSIS

Height of the Water in the Inverted Glass

	Height of Water in Glass (mm)	Fractional Volume	Change in Appearance of Steel Wool Pad
Time = 0			original appearance
Time = 10 minutes			
Time = 20 minutes			
Time = 30 minutes			
Time = ~24 hours			

Total height of the glass (T) = _____ **mm**

(continued)

The Chemical Composition of Air (continued)

❓ CONCLUDING QUESTIONS

1. Why does the water in the glass rise? _____

    _____

2. Oxygen is about one fifth of the volume of air. Compare this number to the fractional volume of the space occupied by the water in the glass at the end of your experiment. Are these numbers roughly in agreement? Why should they be? If they aren't, why not?

    _____

    _____

    _____

3. What, if anything, changed in the appearance of the steel wool? Where else have you seen a similar color?

    _____

    _____

4. Why aren't new steel wool pads rusty when you take them out of the box?

    _____

    _____

EXTENSION From your data, plot the fraction of the volume of the glass occupied by water on the vertical axis against time on the horizontal axis. Use a sheet of graph paper or a computer graphing program, if available. Assuming that all of the oxygen in the air in the glass will be used up in this experiment, use the graph you've made to estimate how long this should take.

🌩 Follow-up Activities 🌩

1. With all the oxidation going on in the atmosphere, oxygen would be quickly used up if it were not being continually produced. Research where oxygen in the atmosphere comes from. There is no detectable oxygen in the atmosphere of any planet or moon in the solar system except Earth. What does this suggest (but not prove!)?

2. Iron, which rusts easily, is the main ingredient in steel. The metal tableware that you eat with every day is probably made from steel. Even when its surface is very clean, this tableware doesn't rust when exposed to air because it is "stainless steel." Research the manufacture of stainless steel. Find out what it is made of, and why it resists rust.

Scattering of Light by Small Particles: A Demonstration Using Milky Water

 ## INSTRUCTIONAL OBJECTIVES

Students will be able to

- demonstrate that light is scattered by small particles in an otherwise clear medium.
- formulate hypotheses about what will happen if the conditions of the experiment are changed.

 ## NATIONAL SCIENCE STANDARDS ADDRESSED

Students demonstrate an understanding of

- interaction of energy and matter.
- cause and effect.
- identifying variables.

Students demonstrate scientific inquiry and problem-solving skills by

- framing questions.
- working in teams to collect and share information and ideas.

Students demonstrate effective scientific communication by

- arguing from evidence and data.

ADAPTATIONS FOR HIGH AND LOW ACHIEVERS

High Achievers: High achievers should be encouraged to do the Extension and Follow-up activities.

Low Achievers: Review the material prior to the experiment.

 ## MATERIALS

- Milk (preferably skim), about 1 oz
- Two clear, uncolored water glasses or glass (not plastic) beakers
- Strong (krypton-bulb) flashlight with fresh batteries (available in any hardware or discount store)
- Two sheets of white paper
- Teaspoon

 = Safety icon

HELPFUL HINTS AND DISCUSSION

Time frame: 40 minutes, or one class period
Structure: Groups of two or three students
Location: In class or at home

Step 3 is included to make sure that the difference in results between the two glasses of water is not due to some extraneous factor, such as the color or thickness of the glasses. If there appears to be a significant difference in transmission through clear water in the two glasses, it is likely because one of them is thicker or a different color glass than the other. Therefore, try to find two more similar glasses.

SCORING RUBRIC

Full credit should be given to students who answer the Concluding Questions accurately and in complete sentences. Extra credit should be given to students who complete the Extension or Follow-up activities. The quiz can be scored from 1 to 4 correct.

 ## INTERNET TIE-IN   http://match.ucr.edu/home/baez/physics/blue_sky.html

 ## QUIZ   Choose the correct word to complete each of the following sentences:

1. Light transmitted through a scattering medium like milky water is _____ than the original beam of light.
2. Light scattered out of a beam of light by milky water is _____ than the original beam.
3. The effect of scattering is _____ as you add more scattering particles.
4. The amount of scattering is _____ as the wavelength of light increases.

    (a) redder   (c) greater
    (b) bluer   (d) less

Scattering of Light by Small Particles: A Demonstration Using Milky Water

 BEFORE YOU BEGIN

White light consists of waves of all colors. Traveling through empty space, a light beam containing all colors will retain all colors and continue to travel in the same direction. But, if that light beam should pass through a medium containing small particles, an effect called **scattering** can occur. Some light waves will bounce off the small particles and change direction, while others will not be affected. The amount of scattering depends on the relative sizes of the particles and the wavelength of the light being scattered. If the particles are **large** compared with the wavelength of light, then they will act like tiny mirrors, reflecting all wavelengths of light equally. The color of the scattered light will be the same as that of the original beam. If the scattering particles are **small** compared with the wavelength of light, then the amount of scattering will depend on the wavelength of the light. Shorter wavelengths (bluer light) are scattered more than longer wavelengths (redder light). This results in scattered light that is bluer than the original beam, and transmitted light that is redder than the original beam. The amount of scattering also increases as the number of particles increases. As we will see in another activity, scattering produces observable effects in the atmosphere. In this activity, we observe the effects of scattering firsthand.

 MATERIALS

- Milk (preferably skim), about 1 oz
- Two clear, uncolored water glasses or glass (not plastic) beakers

 **= Safety icon**

- Strong (krypton-bulb) flashlight with fresh batteries (available in any hardware or discount store)
- Two sheets of white paper
- Teaspoon

 PROCEDURE

1. Fill the two glasses with tap water so that they are about $\frac{3}{4}$ full.

2. Place the glasses next to each other on a flat work area. Tape a sheet of white paper to a vertical surface behind the glasses.

3. Darken the room as much as possible. Shine the flashlight horizontally through each glass in turn so that the light falls onto the sheet of paper. (See Diagram 1.) This light, which is traveling in the same direction as the original beam, is **transmitted** light. Check to see that the color of the transmitted light is the same for each glass. If it is not, try again with glasses that are more similar. Turn the lights back on.

4. Put about $\frac{1}{4}$ teaspoon of the milk into one of the glasses and stir. Wait a minute or two for the water in the glass to settle down.

5. Again, darken the room and shine the flashlight horizontally through each of the glasses in turn. Observe the sheet of paper, then record your observations in the Data Collection table. Compare the color and brightness of the light transmitted through the milky glass and the plain glass. Turn the lights back on.

(continued)

Scattering of Light by Small Particles: A Demonstration Using Milky Water *(continued)*

6. Place a sheet of paper over the open tops of the two glasses (the glasses should be close enough together to do this with one sheet).

7. Again, darken the room. Shine the flashlight horizontally through each of the glasses in turn, exactly as you did in steps 3 and 5. This time, observe and record the color and brightness of the light coming out of the top of the milky glass compared with the plain glass. This light, which has been redirected out of the original beam, is **scattered** light. Be sure the flashlight beam itself is not aimed upward to fall on the second sheet of paper. Turn the lights back on.

EXTENSION Add another full teaspoon of milk to the milky glass and repeat the experiment. What's different this time? Now recall the appearance of a regular glass of milk without added water. Does it show any of the effects you saw in this experiment? Why or why not? (*Hint:* Think about what happens as the beam of light tries to pass through an increased number of scattering particles.)

Diagram 1

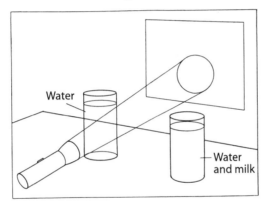

Water

Water and milk

✎ DATA COLLECTION AND ANALYSIS

Observations

	Water-only Glass	**Water-and-milk Glass**
Step 5: color and brightness of light transmitted through glass		
Step 7: color and brightness of light from top of glass		

(continued)

Scattering of Light by Small Particles: A Demonstration Using Milky Water *(continued)*

Milk is a suspension of small solid particles in water. From the observations you have made, what do you conclude is the effect of these particles on the amount and color of transmitted light? What happens to the light that the particles scatter out of the original beam? Which color light (red or blue) is more susceptible to scattering by small particles?

 CONCLUDING QUESTIONS

1. What are the two possible results when a ray of light strikes small particles suspended in a clear medium?

   _____

   _____

   _____

   _____

2. What color of visible light is scattered most strongly? Least strongly? _____

   _____

3. When some of the light is removed from a beam by small particles, does the remaining light appear redder or bluer than the original?

   _____

🌩 Follow-up Activities 🌩

1. Try this experiment with substances other than milk added to water. Record your findings.

2. Take two chalkboard erasers and load them up with chalk dust by erasing many chalkboards. After the erasers are prepared, set up your flashlight on a table to point horizontally. Dim the room lights and turn on the flashlight. First, standing in front of the flashlight, clap the erasers together to create a chalk-dust cloud. Look at the flashlight through the cloud and note the color of the beam. When the chalk dust has settled, stand beside the flashlight. Clap the erasers together again, this time looking at the reflected light from the chalk-dust cloud. Note its color. Compare these results with your results from the milky water experiment. Are the results consistent? (Be sure to clean up any mess made by the chalk dust!)

   ✋ **Do not do this activity if you have asthma or other respiratory problems.**

INSTRUCTIONAL OBJECTIVES

Students will be able to

- explain the phenomenon of the blue sky as an example of light scattering.
- demonstrate that the amount of atmospheric scattering increases as the wavelength of light decreases (blue light scatters more than red light).
- record data in a data table.
- draw conclusions based on data.

NATIONAL SCIENCE STANDARDS ADDRESSED

Students demonstrate an understanding of

- interaction of energy and matter.
- cause and effect.
- relevant concepts to explain observed phenomena.

Students demonstrate scientific inquiry and problem-solving skills by

- framing questions.
- working in teams to collect and share information and ideas.

Students demonstrate effective scientific communication by

- arguing from evidence and data.

ADAPTATIONS FOR HIGH AND LOW ACHIEVERS

High Achievers: High achievers should be encouraged to do the Extension and Follow-Up activities.

Low Achievers: Review the material, particularly the mathematical concepts, prior to the experiment.

MATERIALS

For each group:

- Six-sided playing die
- Red and blue counters or tokens to represent red and blue light waves (15 each). The tokens can be small squares or circles cut out of red and blue paper.

= Safety icon

HELPFUL HINTS AND DISCUSSION

Time frame: 40 minutes, or one class period
Structure: Groups of two or three students
Location: In class

In this activity, students will use tokens representing red and blue light particles to demonstrate the scattering of light that makes the sky blue. Step 2 in the Procedure section should create a "sky" pile with only slightly more blue than red tokens.

In step 3, the final remaining "sunlight" pile should contain noticeably fewer tokens than students started with and many more red than blue tokens. The "sky," or scattered light pile, should be much richer in blue tokens.

Remind students never to look at the sun directly.

SCORING RUBRIC

Full credit should be given to students who answer the Concluding Questions correctly and in complete sentences. Extra credit should be given to students who complete the Extension or Follow-Up activities. The quiz can be scored from 1 to 4 correct.

INTERNET TIE-INS

http://mpfwww.jpl.nasa.gov/default.html
http://mpfwww.jpl.nasa.gov/ops/prm-thmb.html
http://www.naoj.org/subaruimage/jpg/cfht.jpg
http://www.naoj.org/subaruimage/jpg/mko.jpg
http://www.ifa.hawaii.edu/mko/

QUIZ

Which, if any, of the following statements are true?

1. Some sunlight bounces off air molecules in the atmosphere on its way to our eyes.
2. Small particles scatter blue light more than they do red light.
3. Blue light taken out of a beam of sunlight by the atmosphere can never be seen by an observer on the surface of the earth.
4. Direct sunlight gets redder as it goes through more atmosphere.

Name _____   Date _____

Scattering of Sunlight in the Atmosphere: A Light Lottery

 BEFORE YOU BEGIN

   Why is the sky blue? The blue color of a clear sky is the result of the interaction between sunlight, which contains all the colors, and the air molecules in our atmosphere. The air molecules, which are much smaller than the wavelengths of visible light from the sun, scatter the incoming sunlight. In other words, light waves of various colors from the sun encounter air molecules and bounce off them in different directions like billiard balls. The light waves get scattered many times, and eventually come toward your eyes. Since the light waves have been scattered so much, they no longer come from the direction of the sun. Therefore, the entire sky is filled with light. This scattering is strongest for blue-violet light, and gets progressively weaker for green, yellow, and orange. Scattering is weakest for red light. Since the blue-violet light gets scattered the most, the color of the sky appears to be blue.

 MATERIALS

- Six-sided playing die
- Red and blue counters or tokens to represent red and blue light waves (15 each). The tokens can be small squares or circles cut out of red and blue paper

 = Safety icon

 PROCEDURE

1. Mix all the tokens into one pile. This combination of red and blue tokens represents a white ray of sunlight containing equal amounts of red and blue light.
2. Roll the die once for each token in the sunlight pile. For each **red** token, if a **6** is rolled, then the token is removed and put in another pile. This second pile represents the scattered light we see from the sky. If any number other than **6** is rolled, move the red token to a new third pile representing the remaining sunlight. For each **blue** token, if a **5** or **6** is rolled, the token goes to the "sky" pile. If any number other than 5 or 6 is rolled, the token is placed in the remaining "sunlight" pile. Roll the die 30 times—once for each token. Record in the Data Collection and Analysis section the number of tokens of each color in the remaining sunlight pile, and the number of tokens of each color in the scattered light, or sky, pile.
3. Repeat the process starting with the tokens in the remaining sunlight pile three more times. At the end of each trial, again record the number of sunlight and sky tokens.

(continued)

Name _____   Date _____

Scattering of Sunlight in the Atmosphere: A Light Lottery (continued)

DATA COLLECTION AND ANALYSIS

	Sunlight		Sky	
	Red	Blue	Red	Blue
Start	15	15	0	0
Trial 1				
Trial 2				
Trial 3				
Trial 4				

CONCLUDING QUESTIONS

1. What are the final numbers of red and blue tokens in the sunlight, or original, pile? _____

2. What are the final numbers of each in the sky, or scattered light, pile? _____

_____

3. How does your result explain why the sky is blue? _____

_____

4. Explain why the astronauts on the moon could see stars in the sky while the sun was up. _____

_____

5. What would the sky look like if atmospheric scattering were stronger for red light than for blue light? _____

EXTENSION Draw a diagram showing the different amounts of atmosphere that a beam of sunlight must travel through at noon and at sunset. Relate this to the color of the sun itself at those times. **Never look directly at the sun** (with or without binoculars or a telescope).

🌩 Follow-up Activities 🌩

1. Imagine you are in a rocket ship that is launched straight up into the sky. Describe the change in the appearance of the daytime sky as you start from sea level and travel straight up through the atmosphere until you are in space.

2. Mars' atmosphere is about 100 times thinner than Earth's. Suspended in the atmosphere are reddish dust particles from the planet's windswept surface. Find a picture of Mars from the Mars Pathfinder mission that shows the Martian sky. (Your teacher will suggest Internet locations.) What color is the sky on Mars? Can you think of an explanation for this? Finally, describe what you think the Martian sky would look like if the dust in Mars' atmosphere were removed. Name a place on Earth where the sky might look similar to a dustless Martian sky.

INSTRUCTIONAL OBJECTIVES

Students will be able to

- show that the atmosphere exerts a force on everything immersed in it.
- demonstrate that unequal pressure results in a net force.
- draw conclusions based on observations.
- record data in a data table.
- draw conclusions based on data.

 ## NATIONAL SCIENCE STANDARDS ADDRESSED

Students demonstrate an understanding of

- the net effect of balanced and unbalanced forces.
- effects of pressure.

Students demonstrate scientific inquiry and problem-solving skills by

- framing questions.
- working in teams to collect and share information and ideas.
- recognizing sources of bias in data.

Students demonstrate effective scientific communication by

- arguing from evidence and data.

 ## MATERIALS

- Water glass (may be glass or plastic)
- Playing card a little larger than the diameter of the opening of the glass
- Bowl or pot that is at least 5 cm taller than the glass
- Ten or more straight plastic drinking straws
- Black vinyl electrical tape (preferred) or transparent tape
- Scissors
- Ruler or meterstick
- Chair or step stool that can safely support a student's weight

HELPFUL HINTS AND DISCUSSION

Time frame: 40 minutes, or one class period
Structure: Individuals or groups of two to three students
Location: In class or at home

In this activity, students will demonstrate how imbalances in air pressure affect objects.

In step 1 of Part B, make sure that the students have made a super-straw that is airtight. Check the joints to see that they are smooth and well sealed.

open end

Step 1

open end

Step 2

Step 3

ADAPTATIONS FOR HIGH AND LOW ACHIEVERS

High Achievers: High achievers should be encouraged to do the Extension and Follow-Up activities. High achievers should be encouraged to come up with their own demonstrations of the effects of air pressure. Possibilities might include:

- blowing with a straw over a strip of paper that is taped to a table along one narrow end and allowed to hang down over the end of the table. The lowered air pressure produced by blowing over the paper will create a net force upward, and the strip of paper should stick straight out from the table.

- blowing up a balloon and releasing it without tying the stem off. This will demonstrate that the increased pressure inside the balloon forces some air out. The exhaust of air provides a force that propels the balloon around the room.

- placing a tied-off inflated balloon into a freezer for a few minutes. The cooled air in the balloon will exert less pressure, and the balloon will shrink. The balloon will expand as it warms back up to room temperature.

Low Achievers: Review the material prior to the experiment. Ask the high achievers to help these students.

SCORING RUBRIC

Full credit should be given to students who correctly complete the data table and who write their descriptions in complete sentences. Extra credit should be given to students who complete the Extension or Follow-up activities. The quiz can be scored from 1 to 4 correct.

 **INTERNET TIE-IN**   http://ww2010.atmos.uiuc.edu/(Gh)/guides/mtr/pw/prs/def.rxml

 QUIZ
1. What is the force per unit area exerted by a fluid called?
2. How does atmospheric pressure change with increasing altitude?
3. At sea level, can the atmosphere support a column of water that is one meter high?
4. When you begin to sip water through a straw, how does the air pressure at the top of the straw compare with the surrounding air pressure?

Name _____ Date _____

Atmospheric Pressure: The Ocean of Air Around Us

 BEFORE YOU BEGIN

The atmosphere is a sea of air, and we are immersed in it just as a fish is immersed in the ocean. Both water and air are **fluids**. Fluids have the property of exerting a pressure in all directions on all objects within them. **Pressure** is defined as **force per unit area**. The value of the pressure at any point in a fluid depends on the weight of the fluid above that point. Therefore, air pressure decreases as you climb a mountain, and water pressure increases as you swim deeper below the surface. For example, at sea level our bodies are subjected to air pressure of about 10^5 newtons per square meter, or 14.7 pounds per square inch. At an altitude of 5,000 meters, air pressure is only 7.9 pounds per square inch, about half that at sea level. We don't generally notice the air pressure on our bodies because it acts on us both inside and out, and the resulting force is balanced.

How can we sense air pressure in action? One way is to replace it with a lower pressure on one side of an object. That's just what we will do in this activity.

 ## MATERIALS
- Water glass (may be glass or plastic)
- Playing card a little larger than the diameter of the opening of the glass
- Bowl or pot that is at least 5 cm taller than the glass
- Ten or more straight plastic drinking straws
- Black vinyl electrical tape (preferred) or transparent tape
- Scissors
- Ruler or meterstick
- Chair or step stool that can safely support a student's weight

 ## PROCEDURE

PART A

1. Fill the bowl or pot with water. Submerge the glass in the water right-side up, making sure that no air remains in the glass. Now invert the glass, keeping it completely under the water.
2. With the glass still under water, slip the card into the water and cover the opening of the glass.
3. Holding the glass upside down with one hand and holding the card flat against the opening of the glass with the other, slowly lift them both out of the water. Let go of the card. Describe what happens in Table A.

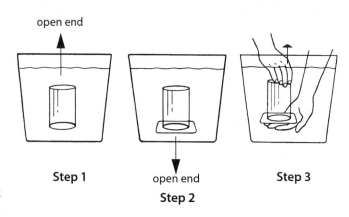

Step 1

open end
Step 2

Step 3

(continued)

Atmospheric Pressure: The Ocean of Air Around Us *(continued)*

EXTENSION Atmospheric pressure at sea level is approximately equal to the pressure at the bottom of a column of water about 10 meters high. As a thought experiment, suppose that the glass were as tall as Mt. Everest—about 7,900 meters high. Ignoring problems such as finding an adequate bowl, how do you think this experiment would turn out if you did it using a 7,900-meter glass? Why?

PART B

1. Tape together individual plastic drinking straws to make a "super-straw" about 1.5 meters long. Be sure that the taped joints between the straws are smooth and completely sealed. The super-straw must be airtight for this experiment to work properly.

2. Fill the glass with water and place it on the floor. Stand on a sturdy chair or step stool while another student steadies it for safety.

3. Now try to sip water from the glass through the super-straw. Make sure to keep the super-straw vertical, and use one long sip on a single breath. *Do not* use a series of small sips to "walk" the water up the straw.

4. If you did not succeed, cut the super-straw shorter in 2-cm steps until you do succeed in sipping water up the straw in a single breath. Note the length of the super-straw at this point in the table on page 22.

   If you did succeed the first time, add one or more straws to the length of the super-straw until you can no longer get a drink. Then cut off 2-cm pieces until you can again. Note that super-straw length in the table below. Be careful to keep the straw vertical.

EXTENSION No one can sip water up through a 20-meter long straw from a glass on the surface of the earth. Why?

5. Now have the other students in your group (or family members if at home) repeat steps 1 to 4. Record the length of the longest straw each person can sip water through. Remember, take one long sip on a single breath and don't walk the water column up the straw.

DATA COLLECTION AND ANALYSIS

Table A   **Observations**

Step 4: glass full of water with the card over it is removed from the water	

(continued)

Atmospheric Pressure: The Ocean of Air Around Us *(continued)*

Table B   Record the maximum height at which each student succeeds in drinking water through the super-straw.

Student 1	
Student 2	
Student 3	

 CONCLUDING QUESTIONS

1. What do you think would have happened in Part A if you did not have the card in place when you lifted the upside-down glass out of the bowl?

   _____

   _____

2. Why did the card prevent this from happening? (*Hint:* What *must* be true about the pressure in the glass compared with the pressure outside the glass?)

   _____

   _____

3. What are you doing to the pressure of the air at the top of the straw when you sip water?

   _____

   _____

4. There is a limit to how low a pressure you can create when you sip, depending on your lung size, training, health, etc. How does this explain your observations in Part B?

   _____

   _____

🌳 Follow-up Activities 🌳

1. Repeat Part A of this experiment with several glasses of different widths, making sure that you have a card large enough to cover the opening in each case. What effect do you expect the width of the glass to have on your results?

2. List some common examples of objects or devices that either change or utilize air pressure. (*Hint:* Think about things that do not function properly if they are not airtight.)

Structure of the Atmosphere

 ## INSTRUCTIONAL OBJECTIVES

Students will be able to

- describe how air density changes with increasing altitude.
- describe how temperature changes with increasing altitude in the troposphere.
- graph data from a table.

 ## NATIONAL SCIENCE STANDARDS ADDRESSED

Students demonstrate an understanding of

- energy in the earth's system: weather.
- structure and properties of matter: density.
- interaction of energy and matter.

Students demonstrate scientific inquiry and problem-solving skills by

- using relevant concepts to explain phenomena.

Students demonstrate effective scientific communication by

- representing data and results in multiple ways.
- arguing from evidence and data.

 ## MATERIALS

- Pen or pencil
- Two 8.5" × 11" sheets of graph paper ruled in centimeter and millimeter divisions
- Ruler or other straightedge
- Calculator (Extension)

HELPFUL HINTS AND DISCUSSION

Time frame: 40 minutes, or one class period
Structure: Individuals
Location: In class or at home

ADAPTATIONS FOR HIGH AND LOW ACHIEVERS

High Achievers: Encourage high-achieving students to do the Extension and Follow-Up activities. Review with them the concepts of area under a graph and value estimation.

Low Achievers: Review the concept of a two-dimensional (*X-Y*) graph. Discuss how to read a data table and plot data on a graph, including how to choose the scale of each axis.

SCORING RUBRIC

Full credit should be given to students who have correctly graphed the data, and who have answered the Concluding Questions accurately and in complete sentences. Extra credit should be awarded to students who do the Extension or Follow-Up activities. The quiz can be scored from 1 to 4 correct.

 ## INTERNET TIE-INS

http://www-astro.physics.uiowa.edu/~jdf/lec22/node3.html
http://trc.dfrc.nasa.gov/shape/TCU/atmosint.htm
http://daac.gsfc.nasa.gov/CAMPAIGN_DOCS/ATM_CHEM/atmospheric_structure.html
http://www.bms.abdn.ac.uk/undergraduate/stdatm4.htm

 ## QUIZ

1. Where in the atmosphere is the thermosphere located?
2. Describe the variation of temperature with altitude in the troposphere.
3. How does the density of the atmosphere change with altitude?
4. Why is the temperature usually cooler on a mountain than in a nearby valley?

Name _____ Date _____

Structure of the Atmosphere

 BEFORE YOU BEGIN

The properties of Earth's atmosphere do not remain the same as you move upward from the surface of the earth. Atmospheric pressure, temperature, density, and composition all change with altitude. For example, both the pressure and density of the atmosphere decrease as altitude increases. In this exercise, you will learn about density and temperature changes in the atmosphere.

Earth's atmosphere can be divided into layers. Each layer is characterized by whether the temperature rises or falls with increasing altitude. The lowest layer, the one in which we live, is called the **troposphere**. The troposphere is where nearly all weather occurs. You may have noticed that even on a summer day, the air is usually cooler on a mountain than it is down below. The air in the troposphere receives its heat from the ground, so the higher above the ground you go, the cooler the air becomes. The temperature in the troposphere decreases at a rate of about 6.5°C per kilometer above the surface. Above the troposphere lies the **stratosphere**. The temperature in the stratosphere rises with altitude. Next is the **mesosphere**, where temperature again falls with altitude. The highest layer of the atmosphere is the **thermosphere**, where temperature rises with altitude. In these layers, factors other than heat from the ground influence the behavior of the air temperature with altitude.

 MATERIALS

- Pen or pencil
- Two 8.5" × 11" sheets of graph paper ruled in cm and mm divisions
- Ruler or other straightedge
- Calculator (Extension)

 PROCEDURE

PART A

Data Table 1 gives the measured density of the atmosphere at different altitudes on a particular day. The densities are scaled so that the value at sea level is 1,000 (the actual units do not matter).

1. On one sheet of graph paper, plot the air density as a function of altitude. Hold the graph paper with the long side vertical, and use the vertical edge for the density axis. Use the horizontal axis for altitude. Using the straightedge, connect the plotted points with straight lines.

2. Estimate and mark on your graph the altitude at which the density of the atmosphere falls to half its value at sea level (0 km altitude).

(continued)

   Walch Hands-on Science Series: Atmosphere and Weather

Structure of the Atmosphere *(continued)*

PART B

Data Table 2 gives the temperature of the atmosphere at different altitudes.

1. Using the values in Data Table 2 and the second sheet of graph paper, plot air temperature as a function of altitude. Hold the graph paper with the long side vertical, and use the vertical edge for the temperature axis. Use the horizontal axis for altitude. Using the straightedge, connect the plotted points with straight lines.

2. Notice that the temperature does not constantly increase or decrease. It changes from increasing to decreasing or decreasing to increasing several times. Mark on the graph all the altitudes where the temperature reverses its behavior.

3. Using the information in the Before You Begin section, label the troposphere, the stratosphere, the mesosphere, and the thermosphere directly on the graph.

Data Table 1

Altitude (km)	Density (0 km = 1,000)
0	1000
10	251
20	53
30	16

Data Table 2

Altitude (km)	Temperature (°C)
0	14
10	−47
20	−58
30	−47
40	−22
50	−2
60	−19
70	−57
80	−93
90	−86
100	−53

(continued)

Structure of the Atmosphere *(continued)*

 EXTENSION You can see from your graph in Part A that the density of air falls off sharply as altitude increases, so most of the atmosphere is located close to the ground. From your graph, find the fraction of the atmosphere up to any particular altitude by estimating the area under the curve you have drawn, going from 0 km (the surface) to that altitude. One way to do this is by counting square-centimeter boxes. Enter your results directly in the third column of Table 1 below. The entry for 0 km is zero square cm (think about why!) and is already entered for you. Take 30 km as the "top" of the atmosphere, so that the area under the curve from 0 km to 30 km represents the total mass of the atmosphere. Find the fraction of the atmosphere lying beneath 10 km and 20 km by dividing those areas by the total area under the graph from 0 to 30 km. Enter these in the last column.

 DATA COLLECTION AND ANALYSIS

PARTS A and B. Write your answers directly on the graph paper.

Table 1 (for Extension)

Altitude (km)	Density (0 km = 1,000)	Total up to This Altitude	
		AREA (sq cm)	**FRACTION**
0	1000	0	0
10	251		
20	53		
30	16	**Total**	1.00

❓ CONCLUDING QUESTIONS

1. Mt. Everest rises about 9 km above sea level. Estimate the density of air at the top of the mountain as a fraction of the density of air in New York City, which is approximately at sea level. How does this value relate to a serious problem experienced by people who climb to the summit of the mountain?

   _____

   _____

2. At approximately what altitude would you be if you were above 90 percent of the atmosphere?

   _____

3. A jet airliner is flying at an altitude of about 11 km, drawing in outside air for the passengers to breathe. Does this air need to be heated or cooled to keep the passengers comfortable?

   _____

4. What is the approximate density of the atmosphere at the top of the troposphere? (*Hint:* Use your temperature-altitude graph to find the altitude first.)

   _____

(continued)

Structure of the Atmosphere *(continued)*

 EXTENSION The data on density and temperature as functions of altitude given in this exercise are very coarse and approximate. Find more detailed and precise data in the library or on the Web, searching under phrases like "U.S. Standard Atmosphere." Using a computer graphing program, create more accurate plots of density, temperature, and pressure if available. Include data for higher altitudes than those used here. Describe any features not already discussed in this exercise.

 Follow-up Activities

1. Layers of the atmosphere can also be distinguished by their electrical properties. A layer in which some of the atoms and molecules of the air have lost at least one electron is called the **ionosphere**. Research the ionosphere, being sure to include its range of altitudes, effects on human activity, and the reasons why its extent can vary significantly with time and latitude.

2. The atmosphere has no real outer boundary. Even satellites in orbit hundreds of kilometers above Earth are not totally outside the atmosphere. Research the effects of "atmospheric drag" on orbiting satellites, including what happens if the effects of drag are not counteracted by the action of onboard rockets.

Convection: Temperature Differences and the Motion of Air

 INSTRUCTIONAL OBJECTIVES

Students will be able to

- demonstrate that warm air tends to rise while cold air sinks.
- describe how this motion, called convection, drives some winds.
- formulate hypotheses about what will happen if the conditions of the experiment are changed.
- explain why knowledge of the properties of laboratory tools is important to the quality of experimental results.

 NATIONAL SCIENCE STANDARDS ADDRESSED

Students demonstrate an understanding of

- energy in the earth's system.
- cause and effect.

Students demonstrate scientific inquiry and problem-solving skills by

- framing questions.
- using laboratory tools to measure phenomena.

Students demonstrate effective scientific communication by

- arguing from evidence and data.

 MATERIALS

- Thermometer readable to 1 degree Fahrenheit or 0.5 degree Celsius
- Watch or clock that can read seconds
- Scrap paper for "reading time" determination measurements
- Standard household refrigerator/freezer

HELPFUL HINTS AND DISCUSSION

Time frame: 40 minutes
Structure: Individuals
Location: At home

In this activity, students will use thermometers to investigate the movement of columns of cold air. It is important to use a thermometer that reacts quickly to temperature changes. Be sure that each student has access to a good lab-quality thermometer or digital electronic household thermometer. Students also must know how to read a thermometer accurately and precisely. Be sure that they know what the divisions on the temperature scale mean, and that they can read the thermometer to within 1 degree Fahrenheit or 0.5 degree Celsius. Also, make sure that the students are able to define and understand density before doing this activity.

ADAPTATIONS FOR HIGH AND LOW ACHIEVERS

High Achievers: High achievers should be encouraged to do the Extension and Follow-Up activities in step 3.
Low Achievers: Review the material prior to the experiment, particularly how to read a thermometer.

SCORING RUBRIC

Full credit should be given to students who answer all questions accurately and in complete sentences and who correctly complete the data tables. Extra credit should be given to students who complete the Extension or Follow-up activities. The quiz can be scored from 1 to 4 correct.

 INTERNET TIE-IN   http://ww2010.atmos.uiuc.edu/(6h)/guides/mtr/hyd/cond/conv.rxml

 QUIZ   Fill in the correct word in each of the following statements.

1. If the volume of a gas is less dense than its surroundings, it will _____.
2. The density of hot air is _____ than that of cold air.
3. When an air column can no longer move vertically (for example, when it strikes the ground), it then moves horizontally and becomes _____.
4. The rising and falling of air columns of different temperatures is called _____ .

Convection: Temperature Differences and the Motion of Air

  BEFORE YOU BEGIN

A high-density object (such as a marble), when placed in a low-density substance (like water), will sink because of gravity. Similarly, a low-density object (like a helium balloon), will rise in a higher-density substance like air.

A volume of any gas, like air, has a lower density at a higher temperature than an equal volume of that same gas at a lower temperature. If a mass of air is heated or cooled, it forms a rising or falling column of air. The greater the temperature difference between the column of air and its surroundings, the greater the air motion. This air movement, driven by temperature differences between volumes of air, is called **convection**. When this air can no longer move vertically (because it strikes the ground, for example), it then moves horizontally and becomes wind. In this activity, we observe convection and the temperature differences that create it.

 MATERIALS

- Thermometer readable to 1 degree Fahrenheit or 0.5 degree Celsius
- Watch or clock that can read seconds
- Scrap paper for "reading time" determination measurement
- Standard household refrigerator/freezer

 PROCEDURE

1. In order to take accurate readings, you will need to know how long it takes for your thermometer to come to the same temperature as its surroundings.

   (a) To determine this, first put the thermometer in the freezer and close the door. Wait about 5 minutes, then open the freezer. Start timing with the watch or clock, and read the thermometer as quickly as possible before it has a chance to warm up. Then, in Table 1, record the temperature of the thermometer as "temperature in the freezer after 5 minutes."

   (b) Now quickly move the thermometer somewhere in the room at least 2 meters away from the freezer. As the thermometer warms up to room temperature, record on a piece of scrap paper the elapsed time and the temperature about every 10 seconds for 5 minutes. Record the last reading in Table 1 as "last reading of temperature in the room." (If you are using an electronic [digital display] thermometer, record the temperature and the time each time the reading changes.)

   (c) Calculate the difference between the freezer reading and the last room reading, taken at 5 minutes. Record it in Table 1 as "total temperature change." Multiply this value by 0.9, and add it to the freezer reading. Record this number in Table 1, entry *e*.

   (d) Now check your list of readings. Find the time it took for the thermometer to reach this temperature, entry *e*, which is 90 percent of the total temperature change (this will be good enough for our experiment). Record this "reading time" in Table 1.

(continued)

Convection: Temperature Differences and the Motion of Air (continued)

(e) In the following steps, be sure to wait at least one "reading time" to get a good measurement once the thermometer is placed in a different temperature environment. Also, wait at least one "reading time" between measurements for the thermometer to come back to room temperature.

2. With the thermometer held just above the freezer door, open the door about an inch. Wait a "reading time" and record the temperature in Table 2. Place your hand where you held the thermometer and make a note of anything you feel. Close the freezer door for at least 10 minutes, then repeat the procedure with the thermometer held below the freezer door. Be sure to hold the thermometer steady. Again, place your hand where you were holding the thermometer, and make a note of anything you feel.

3. Calculate the difference between the two temperatures you have just measured. Record it in Table 2 below. Put a check mark next to the higher temperature.

DATA COLLECTION AND ANALYSIS

Table 1

(a) temperature in the freezer after 5 minutes	
(b) last reading of temperature in the room	
(c) total temperature change (b−a)	
(d) total temperature change × 0.9 (0.9 × c)	
(e) freezer + (0.9 × total change) (a + d)	
(f) reading time (time after which e is reached)	

Table 2

temperature above the freezer	
temperature below the freezer	
temperature difference	

Describe what you felt when you placed your hand above and below the freezer:

(a) above _____

_____

(b) below _____

_____

(continued)

Convection: Temperature Differences and the Motion of Air *(continued)*

EXTENSION Using the same thermometer, measure and record air temperatures near the floor and the ceiling in one or more rooms in your home or school. If it's winter and the building heat is on, try some locations above or below a steam or hot water radiator. What can you say about air movement in the building? How fast do you think it occurs compared with the freezer experiment? (*Hint:* In which circumstances that you've experienced can you feel the flow of air?)

CONCLUDING QUESTIONS

1. What happens to the cold air in the freezer when you open the door?

   _____

   _____

2. How does this explain the temperature measurements you made?

   _____

   _____

   _____

3. How do you think your measurements would have been affected if you had not taken into account the "reading time" of your thermometer?

   _____

   _____

   _____

🌩 Follow-up Activities 🌩

1. Measure the temperature of the air just above and just below the freezer door with the door closed. These temperatures should be within a degree or two of each other. Why? If you find that the temperatures above and below the door are not similar, what reasons can you think of to explain this?

2. Research the principle of hot-air ballooning and write a brief report.

What Is Weather?

 ## INSTRUCTIONAL OBJECTIVES

Students will be able to

- describe what is meant by the term *weather.*
- understand the observations required to describe weather.

 ## NATIONAL SCIENCE STANDARDS ADDRESSED

Students demonstrate an understanding of

- energy in the earth's system: weather.
- cause and effect.

Students demonstrate scientific inquiry and problem-solving skills by

- acquiring information from multiple sources.
- working individually and in teams to collect and share information and ideas.

Students demonstrate effective scientific communication by

- representing data and results in multiple ways.
- arguing from evidence and data.

 ## MATERIALS

PART A

- Outdoor Celsius thermometer or lab thermometer
- Ruler

 = Safety icon

PART B

- Outdoor Celsius thermometer or lab thermometer
- Whiteboard, flip chart, or overhead transparency and projector

HELPFUL HINTS AND DISCUSSION

Time frame: 5–10 minutes per day for 5 days at home; 20–30 minutes at school (see below)

Structure: Individuals (at home) and collectively (in class)

Location: At home and in class

In this activity, students will collectively and individually compile charts of their weather observations. When the observations for Part A are complete, form three to four groups in class and have the members of each group compare their observations with one another. Try to have each group contain students who live in a variety of areas.

For Part B, assign each student a specific time (at intervals of about an hour) to make his or her observations. You will probably need to extend the observations over several days to give every student a turn. Pick an easily accessible spot for the students to do their observations—preferably a place where an outdoor thermometer is available for their use. If any students live very close to the school (say, within half a kilometer) you may wish to assign them times outside of regular school hours for their observations, which can be made either at school or at home, in order to obtain more nearly continuous time coverage. In that case, be sure that those students have access to an outdoor thermometer (either their own or the school's). 🖐 **Do *not* have the students carry glass laboratory thermometers around the school during the school day.**

When all of the observations have been made, have the students copy their results onto a whiteboard, flip chart, or overhead transparency that you have already prepared. The display should have a table similar to that shown under Data Collection and Analysis, Part B, but with many blank rows for all the students' observations. The students should be able to look at this summary of the class's observations while they answer the Concluding Questions.

<table>
<tr><td>

ADAPTATIONS FOR HIGH AND LOW ACHIEVERS

High Achievers: Encourage these students to do the Extension and Follow-up Activities.

Low Achievers: Review a sample completed weather log with these students to make sure they understand how to observe and how to fill in the log. Have these students practice the procedure of obtaining the data.

</td><td>

SCORING RUBRIC

Full credit should be given to students who have performed all of their assigned observations and answered the Concluding Questions correctly and in complete sentences. Extra credit should be awarded to students who do the Extension and Follow-up activities. The quiz can be scored from 1 to 4 correct.

</td></tr>
</table>

 **INTERNET TIE-INS**   http://ww2010.atmos.uiuc.edu/(Gh)/guides/mtr/home.rxml
http://inspire.ospi.wednet.edu:8001/curric/weather/hsweathr/links.html
http://www.weather.com/twc/homepage.twc

 QUIZ
1. What changing properties of the atmosphere are considered to be weather?
2. Distinguish between weather and climate.
3. True or False: Weather can be predicted with certainty over several days.
4. True or False: Weather phenomena rarely cover large areas of the earth.

Name _____   Date _____

What Is Weather?

 BEFORE YOU BEGIN

"Everybody talks about the weather, but nobody does anything about it," goes an old saying. Yet, before we can do anything about the weather, we need to know what it is and what it isn't.

Suppose that the condition of the atmosphere never changed and was the same everywhere around the surface of the earth. Then there wouldn't be much point in including a weather report in the local newspaper or on the TV news. Every day the report would be exactly the same as the day before: "Clear and calm, with a low of 20 degrees Celsius and a high of 20 degrees here in Springfield, but in Alaska it's clear, calm, and 20 degrees, and in Arizona it's 20 degrees, calm, and clear."

In fact, the condition of the atmosphere *does* change, and in complicated, sometimes violent ways. These changes are what we call **weather**, and they are interesting both for their effects on our lives (snow for sledding, baseball games canceled due to rain, etc.) and because it is very difficult to predict the weather reliably over time. The changing properties of the atmosphere that we consider to be weather include temperature, pressure, humidity, wind speed and direction, cloudiness and the types of clouds present, and the amount and types of precipitation.

Weather is usually considered to include only **short-term changes**, from minutes to months. Longer-term trends in weather are called **climate**. We also usually think of weather as **local**. Conditions can often be quite different only a few kilometers away, although some weather phenomena can cover several states—or even occasionally affect much of the globe.

 **MATERIALS**

PART A
- Outdoor Celsius thermometer or lab thermometer
- Ruler

PART B
- Outdoor Celsius thermometer or lab thermometer
- Whiteboard, flip chart, or overhead transparency and projector

 **PROCEDURE**

PART A

In this activity, you will make your own weather observations. You should observe and record the items in the table at home for five consecutive days during a school week. Be sure to make your observations at about the same time of day for each of the five days. Identify the location of the weather observation by street address, intersection ("Fifth and Main"), neighborhood, or other landmark ("near the train station"), and record the conditions at the time of the observation. Keep the descriptions simple. For example, don't try to identify cloud types (you'll do that in another activity), but use broad descriptions such as "clear" (little or no cloud cover), "partly cloudy" (substantial cloudiness, but some clear blue sky as well), and "cloudy" (completely overcast). Note any interesting condition you observe that is not specifically asked for in the table, such as "I hear thunder" or "the fog is as thick as pea soup" or "it snowed last night" in the Comments section. If there is snow on the

(continued)

What Is Weather? *(continued)*

ground, measure it with the ruler and record your result in the Comments section. These observations will show the kind of variation in weather that occurs from day to day and from place to place.

PART B

To demonstrate the variations in atmospheric conditions that occur over short time spans in a single location, your class will collaborate on observations of the weather at your school. You will make the same observations as before, but each member of the class will be assigned a specific time to make his or her observations. You will then combine your observations to create a single chart.

 DATA COLLECTION AND ANALYSIS

PART A

Record your observations in the table below.

Approximate time of observations:				
Location:				
DAY	Temperature (°C)	Wind (calm, light, strong)	Clouds (clear, partly cloudy, cloudy)	Precipitation (none, or as observed)
Mon.				
Comments:				
Tues.				
Comments:				
Wed.				
Comments:				
Thurs.				
Comments:				
Fri.				
Comments:				

PART B

Record your observations in the table below.

Date and time of observations:			
Location: at school			
Temperature (°C)	Wind (calm, light, strong)	Clouds (clear, partly cloudy, cloudy)	Precipiation (none, or as observed)
Comments:			

(continued)

Name _____ Date _____

 CONCLUDING QUESTIONS

1. Did the weather change much during your five days of observations? Comment on the changes you observed.

   _____

   _____

   _____

2. What was the difference between the highest and lowest temperatures you recorded at home in your five days?

   _____

EXTENSION In an atlas or almanac (or on the Weather Channel), find the average expected daytime temperature at your location during the time of year of your observations. Calculate the average of the five temperature observations you made by adding them up and dividing by five. How does your observed average temperature compare with the predicted temperature?

3. Were there differences in the observations made by students in your group living in different locations? If so, what were they?

   _____

   _____

4. From the collected observations of the weather at school (Part B), how long does it take for substantial weather changes (clear to overcast, dry to raining, cold to warm) to occur?

   _____

   _____

🌩 Follow-up Activities 🌩

1. Continue recording the temperature and sky conditions at home for another week. Compare your readings with those reported in the local newspaper or TV.

2. Contact a local TV meteorologist. Ask him or her to visit your school and talk about weather forecasting and reporting.

3. Look up the record high and low temperatures at your location for the dates of your class observations. How do they compare with the temperatures your class recorded?

Air Masses and Fronts

 INSTRUCTIONAL OBJECTIVES

Students will be able to

- define the concepts of air masses and fronts.
- recognize characteristics of different types of air masses and fronts.
- evaluate properties of data in a table.
- draw conclusions based on data.

 NATIONAL SCIENCE STANDARDS ADDRESSED

Students demonstrate an understanding of

- energy in the earth's system: weather.
- properties of matter: density.

Students demonstrate scientific inquiry and problem-solving skills by

- framing questions.
- using relevant concepts to explain observed phenomena.
- working individually and in teams to collect and share information and ideas.

Students demonstrate effective scientific communication by

- arguing from evidence and data.

 MATERIALS

- Pen or pencil
- 4 fl oz of dark corn syrup
- Rectangular clear plastic or glass open-top container, approximately 4 to 6 cm wide, 10 to 20 cm long, and 2 to 4 cm deep. A plastic drawer from a small, multi-drawer small-parts storage cabinet is ideal.

COLD FRONT

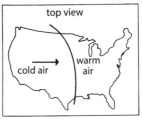
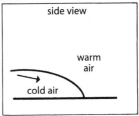

WARM FRONT

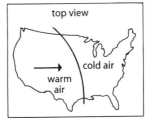
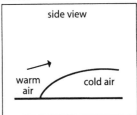

HELPFUL HINTS AND DISCUSSION

Time frame: 40 minutes, or one class period
Structure: Part A: individuals
Part B: pairs
Location: In class or at home

In Part A of this activity, students will identify and sketch the boundaries of warm, cool, and medium fronts based on temperature data in a table. In Part B, students will simulate one front overtaking another.

Review the definitions of air masses and fronts. Also review the concept of density, and the fact that cold air is denser than warm air. Remind students that the second data table in Part A is for the same area as the first data table, but contains later measurements. Students should look for a change in the position of the fronts and air masses they are locating.

ADAPTATIONS FOR HIGH AND LOW ACHIEVERS

High Achievers: Encourage these students to do the Extension and Follow-up activities.

Low Achievers: Prior to the activity, review instructions on how to draw lines indicating boundaries between air masses. Make sure that students understand that they are looking for noticeable differences in temperature across the boundaries. For Part B, pair low achievers with high achievers who can help with the relevant concepts.

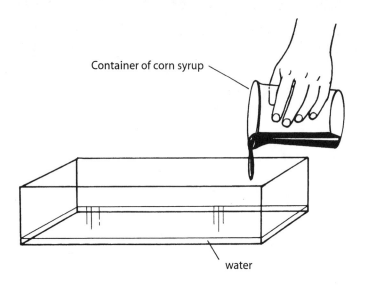

Container of corn syrup

water

SCORING RUBRIC

For Part A, full credit should be given to students who have drawn the location of the fronts correctly on both data tables, and who correctly label the air masses and fronts. For Part B, full credit should be given if at least one of the sketches shows the syrup sliding under the water, if water and syrup are labeled, and if the direction of motion of the syrup is indicated. Extra credit should be given to students who do the Extension of Follow-up activities. The quiz can be scored from 1 to 5 correct.

 **INTERNET TIE-INS**   http://ww2010.atmos.uiuc.edu/(6h)/guides/mtr/af/arms/home.rxml
http://ww2010.atmos.uiuc.edu/(6h)/guides/mtr/af/frnts/home.rxml

 QUIZ   1. What is an air mass?
2. What is the difference between a cold front and a warm front?
3. Does a warm air mass slide under or over a cold air mass it is overtaking?
4. Is a cold air mass denser or less dense than a warm air mass?
5. Why does a cold air mass slide under a warm air mass it is overtaking?

Name _____   Date _____

Air Masses and Fronts

 BEFORE YOU BEGIN

The properties of the air in the atmosphere are not the same everywhere. However, there are broad regions of air with relatively uniform temperature and/or humidity. These regions are known as **air masses**. Air masses move over the surface of the earth and can overtake, be overtaken by, or mix with, other air masses they encounter.

The boundaries between air masses are called **fronts**. Types of fronts are determined by the relative temperatures of the air masses involved. If a warmer air mass is overtaking a colder air mass, it will slide *over* the colder air mass because warm air is less dense than cold air. The boundary between the warm air mass and the cold air mass in a case like this is called a **warm front**. If colder air is overtaking warmer air, the colder air will slide *under* the warmer air, because cold air is denser. The boundary between the two air masses in a case like this is called a **cold front**. In this activity, you will identify and simulate air masses and fronts.

COLD FRONT

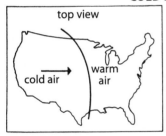

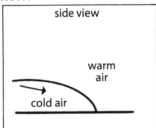

WARM FRONT

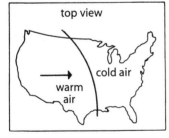

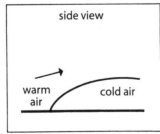

MATERIALS

- Pen or pencil
- 4 fl oz of dark corn syrup
- Rectangular clear plastic or glass open-top container, approximately 4 to 6 cm wide, 10 to 20 cm long, and 2 to 4 cm deep. A plastic drawer from a small, multi-drawer small-parts storage cabinet is ideal.

PROCEDURE

PART A

Data Tables 1 and 2 are grids that represent surface air temperatures in degrees Celsius over a 10-km- × 10-km square area. There are three air masses and two fronts in this area. Data Table 2 represents data taken about 10 minutes after the data in Data Table 1.

1. Examine Data Table 1. Locate and sketch in the boundaries of the three air masses (you may draw directly on the Table). Remember, you are looking for boundaries between areas with noticeably different temperatures.

2. Estimate the average temperature of each of the three air masses and label them in increasing order of temperature: *cool*, *medium*, and *warm*. Remember that these terms are only relative.

(continued)

3. At this point you know which air masses are which, but you don't know what kind of fronts are present. To determine which fronts are present, repeat step 1 for Data Table 2. Notice that the fronts have moved.

Data Table 1

14	13	13	15	13	13	15	14	19	19
13	15	14	14	13	14	15	15	20	20
15	14	14	14	15	15	13	18	19	20
15	15	15	14	15	15	21	20	19	20
14	14	15	15	14	20	19	20	20	19
15	16	14	23	23	24	19	20	19	18
23	23	24	22	22	23	24	21	20	20
22	23	24	23	24	23	23	23	20	19
23	24	23	25	25	24	24	24	23	18
22	24	24	24	25	24	23	23	22	17

Data Table 2

14	13	13	15	13	13	15	14	15	19
13	15	14	14	13	14	15	15	14	20
15	14	14	14	15	15	13	14	19	20
15	15	15	14	15	15	15	20	19	20
14	14	15	15	14	15	23	20	20	19
15	16	14	14	15	24	24	24	19	18
14	15	15	14	22	23	24	21	23	20
15	23	24	23	24	23	23	23	24	24
23	24	23	25	25	24	24	24	23	24
26	25	26	24	23	25	25	23	24	24

PART B

1. Fill the clear container with water to a depth of 3 to 5 millimeters (no deeper!).

2. Work in teams of two. One of you, the *observer*, should position yourself to view the container from the long side, with the water at eye level. Be prepared to sketch what you see.

3. Your partner, the *pourer*, should now begin to pour a steady stream of dark corn syrup into the water at one end of the open container. The pouring should be at a steady rate so that it takes about 20 to 30 seconds to pour out the entire 4 fluid ounces. As this is being done, the observer should observe and sketch the appearance of the boundary between the water and the corn syrup, including its position in the clear container. Try to observe and sketch quickly enough to make two sketches: once early during the pour, and once after the corn syrup is half way poured out of the container. Be sure to note the direction of movement of the corn syrup.

4. About a minute after all the corn syrup has been poured, the observer and the pourer change places. The pourer should now observe and sketch the water–corn syrup boundary.

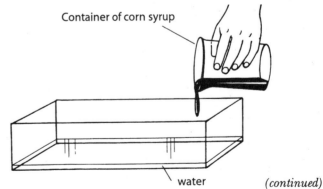

Container of corn syrup

water

(continued)

Air Masses and Fronts *(continued)*

DATA COLLECTION AND ANALYSIS

PART A

Indicate your answers directly in the data tables.

PART B

Sketch your observations in the following boxes. Each box represents the side view of the container through which you viewed the experiment. Be sure to label the water, the corn syrup, and the direction of movement of the corn syrup.

Early in pour

Late in pour

After the pour

CONCLUDING QUESTIONS

1. From the movement of the fronts in Part A and the type of air masses behind them, determine the type of each front (warm or cold). Label it directly in Data Table 2.

2. From its behavior in the experiment, does the corn syrup behave like a warmer or colder air mass than the water? _____

3. Based on your answer to question 2, what kind of front did you make with the water and the corn syrup: warm or cold? _____

4. Why did the corn syrup slide under the water? _____

_____

(continued)

Air Masses and Fronts *(continued)*

 EXTENSION In addition to cold fronts and warm fronts, there are two other kinds of fronts indicated on weather maps: **stationary fronts** and **occluded fronts**. Research the descriptions of these kinds of fronts, and the symbols meteorologists use to indicate the different kinds of fronts on weather maps.

 FOLLOW-UP ACTIVITIES

1. Look at the weather map in today's newspaper (or at a Web site). Notice the fronts indicated on the map. What kind of front is currently closest to your location? What fronts might pass over your location in the next few days?

2. Try Part B with liquids other than corn syrup, such as shampoo and dishwashing liquid. Do they behave in the same way as the corn syrup? Why or why not?

Highs, Lows, and Winds

 ## INSTRUCTIONAL OBJECTIVES

Students will be able to

- explain the concepts of high- and low-pressure areas.
- identify highs and lows on a barometric map.
- evaluate properties of data in a table.

 ## NATIONAL SCIENCE STANDARDS ADDRESSED

Students demonstrate an understanding of

- energy in the earth's system: weather.
- properties of matter: density, pressure.

Students demonstrate scientific inquiry and problem-solving skills by

- identifying variables.
- using relevant concepts to explain observed phenomena.
- working individually and in teams to collect and share information and ideas.

Students demonstrate effective scientific communication by

- arguing from evidence and data.

 ## MATERIALS

For each pair:

- Pen or pencil
- Sheet of paper, 8.5" × 10" or larger
- Vacuum cleaner (preferably canister type or "shop vac")
- Oatmeal or other cylindrical cardboard container
- Duct tape or other similar tape
- Confetti

HELPFUL HINTS AND DISCUSSION

Time frame: 40 minutes, or one class period
Structure: Part A: individuals
                 Part B: pairs
Location: In class or at home

In Part A of this activity, students will locate and label pressure areas based on air pressure values in a table. In Part B, students will simulate the difference in air pressure that results in wind. Review the concept of high- and low-pressure areas. Also review the concept of density, and the fact that cold air is denser than warm air and dry air denser than moist air.

ADAPTATIONS FOR HIGH AND LOW ACHIEVERS

High Achievers: Encourage these students to do the Extension and Follow-up activities.

Low Achievers: Prior to the exercise, review instructions on how to draw lines indicating equal air pressures (isobars). Make sure that the students understand that to find which way the wind blows, they must look for differences in pressure, and that wind moves air from higher to lower pressure areas. For Part B, pair low achievers with high achievers.

SCORING RUBRIC

For Part A, full credit should be given to students who draw the location of the isobars correctly on the data table, label the highs and lows correctly, and answer the Concluding Questions correctly and in complete sentences. For Part B, full credit can be given if the pattern drawn on the paper indicates motion toward the center, and if the area under the oatmeal box is correctly identified as a low-pressure region. Extra credit should be given to students who complete the Extension or Follow-up activities. The quiz can be scored from 1 to 4 correct.

 ## INTERNET TIE-INS
http://ww2010.atmos.uiuc.edu/(Gh)/guides/mtr/fw/prs/lwdef.rxml
http://ww2010.atmos.uiuc.edu/(Gh)/guides/mtr/fw/prs/hghdef.rxml
http://www.usatoday.com/weather/wpress.htm

 ## QUIZ
1. What is a high?
2. Above a low, is the air rising or falling?
3. True or False: Wind blows from lower pressure toward higher pressure areas.
4. True or False: Highs are usually accompanied by precipitation.

Highs, Lows, and Winds

 BEFORE YOU BEGIN

Cold air is denser than warm air. Dry air is denser than moist air. A body of dense air—cold and dry—surrounded by air of lower density—warmer and moister—will fall toward the ground. This compresses the air below. The atmospheric pressure then rises locally, becoming a high-pressure region, or simply a **high**. Such high-pressure regions usually have low humidity and little or no cloudiness. This is because the downward motion of the atmosphere transports cold air (which cannot hold much water) from high altitudes to the earth's surface, warming it in the process and lowering its relative humidity. Highs are usually found in the central regions of air masses, far away from the fronts that form their boundaries.

In a **low**, or low-pressure region, the column of air is rising instead of falling, so the atmospheric pressure near the surface is lowered. Warm, moist air from near the surface (a rising column of air) is cooled off as it rises, often to the point that the water vapor in it condenses to form clouds and precipitation. Unlike highs, lows form in a variety of ways, including local heating, absorption of water vapor by the atmosphere, and most commonly by the collision of air masses at a front. Lows are sometimes called **storm systems**, because they are often accompanied by widespread clouds and precipitation—and sometimes by thunderstorms.

Different pressures at different locations, or **atmospheric imbalances**, cause the atmosphere to try to equalize itself. To accomplish this equalization, the "excess" air moves from an area with high atmospheric pressure toward an area with lower pressure; we call this motion **wind**. Winds usually fan outward from a high, and come together toward a low. The greater the difference in pressure between two nearby locations, the faster the air moves and the stronger the wind. In this activity, you will identify high- and low-pressure regions, and simulate one way in which winds are created.

 MATERIALS

- Pen or pencil
- Sheet of paper, 8.5" × 10" or larger
- Vacuum cleaner (preferably canister type or "shop vac")
- Oatmeal or other cylindrical cardboard container
- Duct tape or other similar tape
- Confetti

 PROCEDURE

PART A

Data Table 1 shows surface air pressures in millibars over a 1,000-km × 1,000-km square area. There may be highs and/or lows in this area.

(continued)

Highs, Lows, and Winds *(continued)*

1. Examine the table. Locate and circle the highest and lowest pressure readings. If you find more than one adjacent location having that value, include it within the circle that you draw. Call these locations you have identified "pressure centers."

2. For each pressure center identified in step 1, go to the next higher or lower pressure in the grid. Draw lines connecting locations of equal pressure, as you would in a connect-the-dots puzzle. Where possible, try to draw closed loops entirely surrounding the previous pressure value. Don't worry if in some places you cannot close the loops and must leave the them open.

3. Repeat step 2 for all remaining pressure values **except 1,000 millibars** (those locations will be left alone). The lines you have drawn are called **isobars**.

4. Label the high- and low-pressure regions you have drawn in Data Table 1.

Data Table 1

1000	1000	1020	1040	1020	1000	1000	1000	1000	1000
1020	1040	1040	1060	1040	1020	1000	1000	1000	1000
1040	1060	1080	1060	1040	1020	1000	1000	1000	*1000*
1020	1040	1060	*1040*	1020	1020	1000	1000	1000	980
1020	*1020*	1040	1020	1000	1000	980	980	980	960
1000	1020	1020	1000	1000	980	*960*	960	940	960
1000	1000	1000	1000	1000	980	960	940	920	940
1000	1000	1000	1000	980	960	940	920	940	960
980	1000	1000	1000	1000	980	960	940	960	980
960	980	1000	1000	1000	1000	980	960	980	1000

PART B

1. Remove the cover of the oatmeal container so that it is open at one end. Cut a hole in the other end and tape the vacuum cleaner hose or nozzle to the hole. Tape a sheet of paper to the floor.

2. One member of your team should hold the open end of the container a centimeter or two above the sheet of paper and turn on the vacuum. That person may want to sit in a chair in order to hold the apparatus steady.

3. The other team member should then place pieces of confetti on the paper near the open end of the oatmeal container. If necessary, adjust the height of the canister or its distance from the confetti so that the vacuum picks up the confetti. When the procedure seems to be working right, place pieces of confetti one by one at various points on the floor around the oatmeal canister. Watch how each one moves, and draw an arrow on the sheet of paper indicating its path. This will make a map of the flow pattern near this artificial "pressure center."

(continued)

Name _____   Date _____

Highs, Lows, and Winds *(continued)*

 DATA COLLECTION AND ANALYSIS

PART A

Write your answers directly on the data table.

PART B

Your observations should be recorded directly on the sheet of paper placed under the container.

 CONCLUDING QUESTIONS

PART A

1. At each of the four locations in italics in Data Table 1, determine the direction of the wind. Draw an arrow from these locations indicating the wind direction.

   _____

   _____

2. Determine which of the four locations referred to in question 1 has the strongest wind. Draw a "+" at this location.

   _____

   _____

EXTENSION Do the following for five consecutive days: Obtain a current local or regional weather map from a newspaper, the Internet, or other source. From the labeled highs, lows, and isobars, try to predict the general direction of the wind in your area. If a high is right over your location, you would predict "no wind." Sometime near the middle of the day, go outside and observe the actual direction of the wind, if any. Compare your predictions with your observations. How often were you correct?

PART B

1. Based on the action of the vacuum cleaner and the pattern you drew on the sheet of paper, is the area under the oatmeal box a high or a low?

EXTENSION Describe how you would need to change the action of the vacuum cleaner to create another kind of pressure region than the one you identified above.

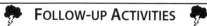 **FOLLOW-UP ACTIVITIES**

The air moving outward from a high does not go in straight lines: it is affected by a force called the Coriolis effect. This force arises from the earth's rotation. In the Northern Hemisphere, it causes the path of a moving object to be deflected to the right of the path it would take if there were no Coriolis effect. Make a sketch that shows the Coriolis effect, with winds moving outward from a high.

Reading a Weather Map

  ## INSTRUCTIONAL OBJECTIVES

Students will be able to

- read a weather map.
- make basic predictions about short-term weather.

NATIONAL SCIENCE STANDARDS ADDRESSED

Students demonstrate an understanding o

- energy in the earth's system: weather.

Students demonstrate scientific inquiry and problem-solving skills by

- acquiring information from multiple sources, including the Internet.

Students demonstrate effective scientific communication by

- arguing from evidence and data.
- representing data in multiple ways.

 ## MATERIALS

For each student:

- Pencil
- U.S. map showing states and major cities

HELPFUL HINTS AND DISCUSSION

Time frame: 40 minutes, or one class period
Structure: Individuals or pairs
Location: In class or at home

In this activity, students will label fronts, make weather forecasts, and use symbols to indicate weather phenomena across maps of the continental United States. Make sure students are familiar with the concepts of highs, lows, and fronts. They should also be reminded that the prevailing winds in the continental United States blow from west to east.

ADAPTATIONS FOR HIGH AND LOW ACHIEVERS

High Achievers: Encourage these students to do the Extension and Follow-up activities.

Low Achievers: Review relevant concepts, such as high- and low-pressure areas, fronts, and their symbols. If the exercise is done in class, ask high achievers to help this group.

SCORING RUBRIC

Full credit should be given to students who properly label the weather fronts, high wind and precipitation areas, who draw reasonable weather features, and whose forecasts make sense. Extra credit can be given to students who complete the Extension or Follow-up activities. The quiz can be scored from 1 to 5 correct.

 ## INTERNET TIE-INS   http://www.intellicast.com
http://www.weather.com

QUIZ

1. True or False: Reliable detailed weather forecasts are available for up to a month ahead. Explain your answer.
2. Why does most weather in the continental United States move from west to east?
3. What features on a weather map indicate strong winds?
4. How does a cold front differ from a warm front?
5. Draw the map symbols for a cold front and a warm front.

Figure 1

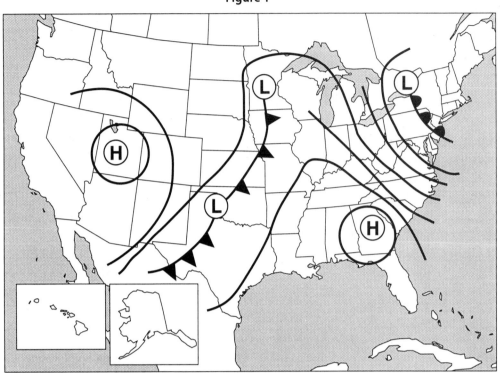

Answer to Data Collection and Analysis, Part B   **Figure 2**

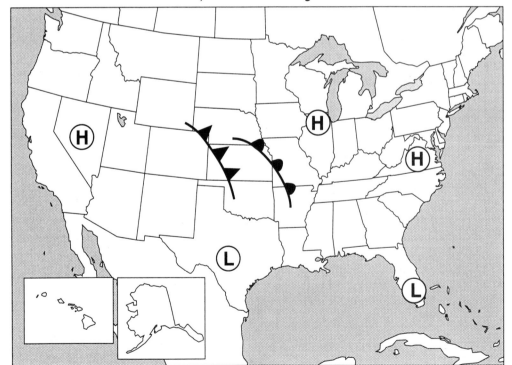

Name _____   Date _____

Reading a Weather Map

 BEFORE YOU BEGIN

You have seen weather forecasts on TV where meteorologists point at a map with odd-shaped lines and unfamiliar symbols and then confidently predict what the weather will be like in your town. Do you ever wonder how they do it? In addition to their years of training and experience, they rely on predictions from powerful computers that digest mountains of detailed weather data from around the country and the world. Even so, these detailed forecasts are reliable only short-term—up to about 48 hours ahead. This is because the atmosphere, continents, and oceans form an extremely complex and somewhat chaotic weather system. By learning a few weather map symbols and remembering some basic weather patterns, you can make **short-term forecasts**.

Prevailing Westerlies

In the continental United States, the basic flow of weather is from **west to east**. This is caused by the **prevailing westerlies**, a wind pattern that circles the globe at our latitude. Air masses and fronts therefore move generally eastward as they come down from Canada or up from Mexico and the Gulf of Mexico. It generally takes weather systems about a week to cross the continental United States.

Isobars, Highs, and Lows

Isobars are lines connecting areas of equal air pressure. When isobars are close together, it indicates a steep change in air pressure—and therefore, strong winds. **Highs** and **lows** are regions where the air pressure is at a maximum or a minimum, respectively. Winds move out from the center of a high in a *clockwise* direction; they move into the center of a low in a *counterclockwise* direction. Highs usually bring fair weather, while precipitation and unsettled weather most often accompany lows. On a weather map, a high-pressure region is represented by the symbol **H**. A low-pressure region is represented by the symbol **L**.

Fronts

Fronts occur where air masses come together. A *warm front* is formed when a warmer air mass overtakes a cooler one. A *cold front* is formed when a cooler air mass overtakes a warmer one. When two air masses that are in contact do not move relative to each other, they create a **stationary front**. And when a cold front overtakes a warm front, lifting the warm air off the ground, an *occluded front* is formed. When a front passes over your location, it generally means a change in the weather that often includes precipitation. Below are the symbols for the different kinds of fronts. On a weather map, the triangles and half-circles are drawn so that they point in the direction the front is moving.

 **MATERIALS**

- Pencil
- U.S. map showing states and major cities

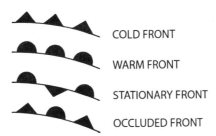

COLD FRONT

WARM FRONT

STATIONARY FRONT

OCCLUDED FRONT

(continued)

Name _____   Date _____

Reading a Weather Map *(continued)*

STUDENT ACTIVITY PAGE

 PROCEDURE

PART A

Figure 1 is a simplified weather map of the continental United States. Refer to it to follow the instructions in the Data Collection and Analysis section.

PART B

Figure 2 is a blank map of the continental United States. Use it to draw the weather features described in the Data Collection and Analysis section.

DATA COLLECTION AND ANALYSIS

PART A

1. Label all the weather fronts in Figure 1, and draw arrows to indicate their directions of movement.

2. Indicate an area where you would predict high winds.

3. Indicate an area where you might expect precipitation.

→ **EXTENSION** A full, detailed description of weather at a particular location is called a ***station model***. Research what is included in a station model report. Gather as much of the required information as you can for your location from the newspaper or the Weather Channel, and create a station model for a particular day.

PART B

1. Using Figure 2, draw high-pressure regions over Nevada, Illinois, and Virginia. Draw low-pressure regions over Texas and Florida.

2. Draw an east-moving warm front from central Nebraska to central Arkansas.

3. Draw an east-moving cold front from central Wyoming to central Oklahoma.

CONCLUDING QUESTIONS

1. Base your answers to questions 1 to 3 on Figure 1. What kind of weather do you predict for Altanta, Georgia, for the next one to two days?

2. Name a large city where there was probably precipitation yesterday.

3. Is the day represented on the map a good day for a picnic in Salt Lake City, Utah?

4. Base your answers to questions 4 to 6 on Figure 2. What kind of weather do you predict for Washington, D.C., for the next one to two days?

5. Describe what will happen if the cold front overtakes the warm front.

6. Name a large city where the weather is likely to be fair for the next one to two days.

(continued)

© 1998 J. Weston Walch, Publisher   50   *Walch Hands-on Science Series: Atmosphere and Weather*

Name ______________________ Date ______________

Reading a Weather Map *(continued)*

STUDENT ACTIVITY PAGE

EXTENSION For one week, collect national weather maps from your local newspaper or printed from the Internet. Assemble them in order (by date) into a "flip book," and flip through them quickly to make a crude animation of the weather. Note the movement of fronts, the development or disappearance of highs and lows, and the spread of precipitation. Make note of any weather news (storms, heat waves, floods, etc.) during the period you are collecting these maps. From all the maps, see if you can identify and track a particular low as it moves across the country. Draw its path on a copy of the blank map (Figure 2) from this activity. Write a short description of what you found, being sure to relate any especially interesting weather events to the features you followed.

FOLLOW-UP ACTIVITIES

Examine some current weather maps at Web sites your teacher gives you. Using these maps, make short-term forecasts for your area and other points of interest.

Figure 1

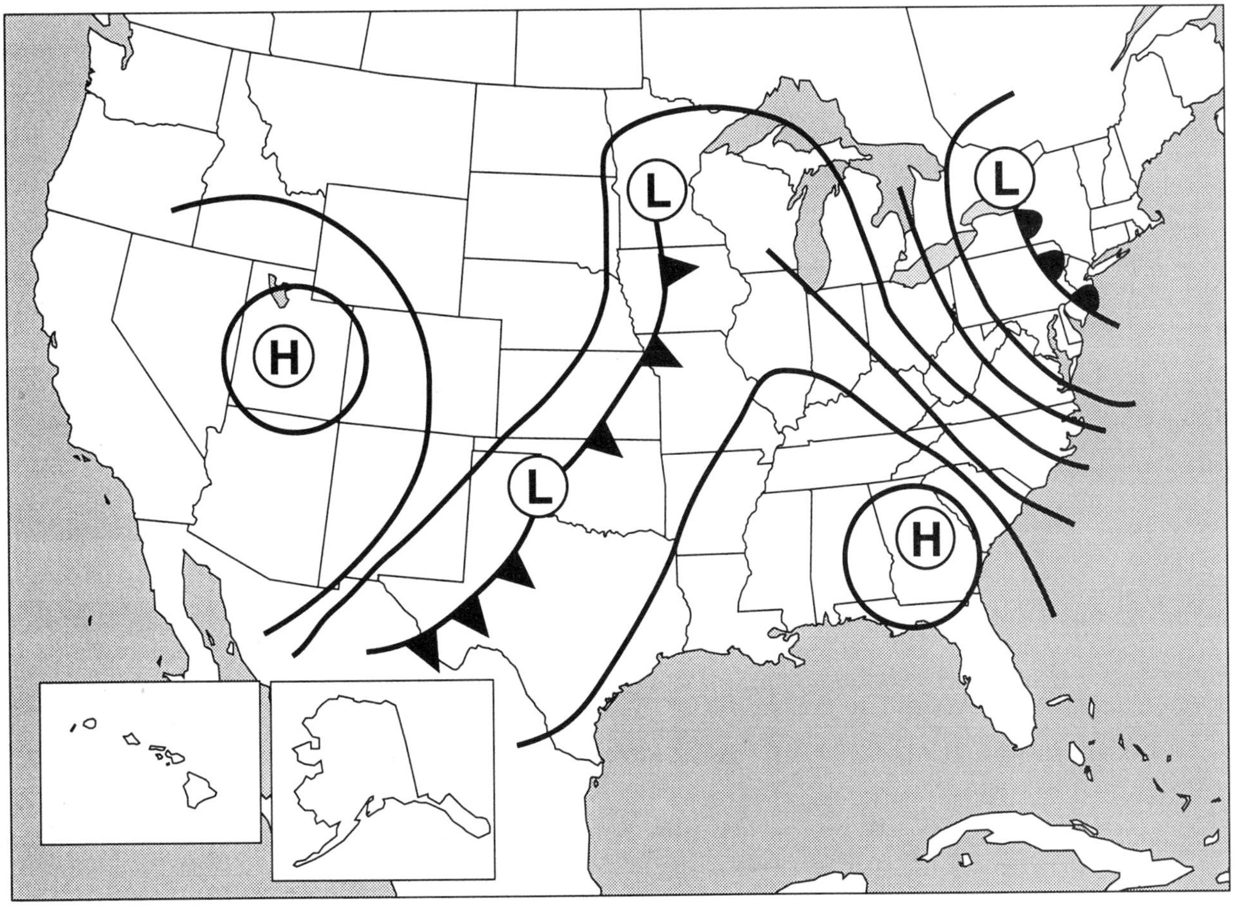

(continued)

Reading a Weather Map *(continued)*

Figure 2

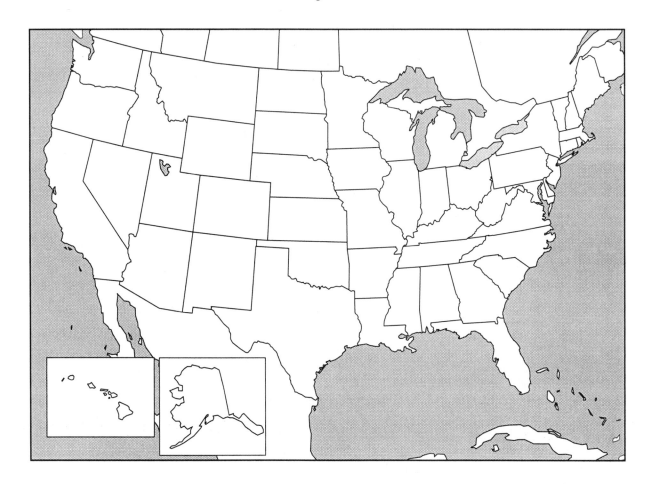

Humidity, Water Vapor, and Clouds

 INSTRUCTIONAL OBJECTIVES

Students will be able to

- demonstrate that air can absorb and release water.
- distinguish between the water-holding capacities of warm and cold air.

 NATIONAL SCIENCE STANDARDS ADDRESSED

Students demonstrate an understanding of

- properties and changes of properties in matter.
- conservation of matter.
- the water cycle.
- energy in the earth's system.

Students demonstrate scientific inquiry and problem-solving skills by

- framing questions and controlling variables.
- using newly learned concepts to explain observations.

Students demonstrate effective scientific communication by

- arguing from evidence and data.

 MATERIALS

- Empty mayonnaise jar (or similar jar) with a tight-sealing lid
- Stove
- Coffee mug or teacup
- Standard household refrigerator/freezer
- Paper towels
- Scissors
- Metric ruler

 Safety icon

HELPFUL HINTS AND DISCUSSION

Time frame: 40 minutes total, over two days
Structure: Individuals
Location: At home

ADAPTATIONS FOR HIGH AND LOW ACHIEVERS

High Achievers: Encourage these students to do the Extension and Follow-up activities.

Low Achievers: Review key concepts and instructions prior to sending the assignment home. Make sure that students understand how to perform the experiment.

SCORING RUBRIC

Full credit should be given if answers and descriptions are correct and given in complete sentences. Extra credit should be awarded to students who complete the Extension or Follow-up activities. The quiz can be scored from 1 to 4 correct.

 INTERNET TIE-IN   http://ww2010.atmos.uiuc.edu/(Gh)/guides/mtr/cld/dvlp/wtr.rxml

 QUIZ   1. Which can hold more water, warm air or cold air?
2. What is the gaseous state of water called?
3. What do we mean by humidity?
4. Is the humidity of air in a freezer high or low?

Name _____   Date _____

  BEFORE YOU BEGIN

Water can exist in the atmosphere in three phases. It can be in the form of a **gas** (water vapor), **liquid** (condensed drops of various sizes), or **solid** (ice particles or crystalline snow). Water goes from liquid to vapor by a process called **evaporation**, driven by heat that comes from the sun.

Although water vapor is not a major component of air, it is an important one. The amounts of nitrogen, oxygen, and most other gases in the air remain fairly constant, yet the water vapor content of air can vary greatly. The maximum amount of water vapor the air can hold depends on temperature: cold air can hold less water vapor than warm air. The amount of water vapor in the air is called **humidity**. Humidity is a factor in many kinds of weather.

Clouds contain water in liquid or solid form. What we call fog is just a cloud at ground level. In this activity, you will investigate the water-holding capacity of air at different temperatures, and you will use this knowledge to make a cloud.

 MATERIALS

- Empty mayonnaise jar (or similar jar) with a tight-sealing lid
- Stove
- Coffee mug or teacup
- Standard household refrigerator/freezer
- Paper towels
- Scissors
- Metric ruler

 Safety icon

 PROCEDURE

PART A

1. Make sure the inside of the jar is clean and dry. Remove the lid from the jar and place the jar in the freezer on its side for about five minutes. This allows the jar to fill with cold, low-humidity air.
2. Dampen a small part of the paper towel with a drop or two of water. Cut a 1-cm square (no larger) out of the damp part of the paper towel. Put the piece of damp paper towel on the underside of the jar lid (it will stick because it is wet); have it ready near the freezer.
3. Open the freezer door. With the jar still inside the freezer, quickly twist the lid on tightly. Then remove the sealed jar from the freezer. Set it aside overnight in a warm (room temperature) place. Do *not* heat the jar.
4. The next day, open the jar and remove the piece of paper towel. Answer the questions under Part A of Data Collection and Analysis.

PART B

1. Open the freezer door about 15 cm (6 inches). Observe how much or how little fog forms inside the freezer. If the space inside the freezer quickly fills with fog, wait for a "dry" day to try this exercise. If there is not much fog, continue to step 2.

(continued)

Humidity, Water Vapor, and Clouds *(continued)*

2. Fill a coffee mug or teacup halfway with *cold* tap water. With the freezer door open about 15 cm, hold the cup inside the freezer for 10 to 15 seconds. Observe and record what you see under Part B of Data Collection and Analysis. Remove the cup from the freezer and empty it.

3. Caution: **Do this step only under adult supervision.** Boil enough water to fill three quarters of the coffee mug or teacup. Open the freezer door, and quickly hold the cup inside the freezer near the bottom as before. Do not do this for more than 15 seconds. Again, observe and record what you see. Remove the cup from the freezer, and put everything back the way you found it.

DATA COLLECTION AND ANALYSIS

PART A

Is the piece of paper towel from the jar wet or dry?

_____

Was there any condensation (water droplets) inside the jar? _____

PART B

What did you see with the cup of cold water in the freezer?

_____

_____

What did you see with the cup of hot water in the freezer?

_____

_____

CONCLUDING QUESTIONS

1. In Part A, what happened to the water in the piece of paper towel? Why? (*Hint:* The air in a freezer has very low humidity because it is so cold.)

_____

2. How does the amount of water vapor above the cup of cold water compare with that above the cup of hot water?

_____

(continued)

Humidity, Water Vapor, and Clouds (continued)

3. What would the phenomenon you see in step 3 of Procedure, Part B, be called if it were in the sky above you?

_____

4. Did you get different results above the cold and hot water in the cup? Why? _____

_____

_____

 EXTENSION Repeat Part A of this experiment *without* placing the jar in the freezer, and with a centimeter of water in the bottom of the jar. Do you get a different result? Why?

 EXTENSION Repeat Part A of this experiment with increasingly large pieces of the damp paper towel. Try increasing the size by 1 cm square each time. See how big a piece of paper towel you can use and still have it dry by the next morning. Why do you think there is a limit to how big a piece of paper towel you can use and still have it dry in the jar overnight?

☁ FOLLOW-UP ACTIVITIES ☁

1. Humidity can be expressed in terms of either the **absolute amount** of water in the air, or the amount **relative to the maximum amount** that the air at a specific temperature can hold. Research and describe the difference between relative and absolute humidity and the types of instruments used to make humidity measurements.

2. Everyone has seen a fogged-up bathroom mirror when a hot shower or hot water faucet has been running. Explain why the mirror gets foggy.

Cloud Types

 ## INSTRUCTIONAL OBJECTIVES

Students will be able to

- identify different cloud types.
- discuss formation of clouds.
- relate cloud types to weather.

 ## NATIONAL SCIENCE STANDARDS ADDRESSED

Students demonstrate an understanding of

- energy transport by convection.
- interaction of energy and matter.
- energy in the earth's system.
- the sun's energy.

Students demonstrate scientific inquiry and problem-solving skills by

- identifying variables.
- using newly learned concepts to explain a variety of observations.
- acquiring information from multiple sources, including the Internet.

Students demonstrate effective scientific communication by

- arguing from evidence and data.
- representing data in multiple ways.

MATERIALS

- Cloud chart showing the different types of clouds—available from, for example, http://www.weathermall.com/wsc/ cldchart.htm
  http://www.isn.net/~wxsense/books.html
- Drawing paper and pencil
- Access to the Internet sites listed
- Individual-size cloud charts the students can take home if available (e.g., try Edmund Scientific); otherwise, they should use their textbooks

 Safety icon

HELPFUL HINTS AND DISCUSSION

Time frame: 5 to 10 minutes per day for at least 5 days for viewing; 40 minutes, or one class period for the Internet portion of the activity

Structure: Individuals

Location: A sky-viewing point, at school or at home

In this activity, students will use what they have learned about cloud types to put together and illustrate a cloud diary. Students should be instructed to choose a place from which to view the sky that will be accessible for several successive days. It would be preferable to have the viewing site outdoors, but if the weather is particularly inclement, a view from a window would be acceptable. The important thing is that the site have a clear view of as much of the sky as possible. The students need not observe at the same time each day.

For students observing outdoors, instruct them not to stay outdoors if they see or hear an approaching thunderstorm. Also warn them not to look directly at the sun.

There may be times when assigning this activity will be impractical; you should check the five-day weather forecast before making the assignment. For example, if the forecast predicts several absolutely clear days with minimal clouds, or if your area is forecast to be completely socked in for several days, then wait before assigning this exercise. Or, as an alternative to the students making their own observations, you could make use of "live" weather images from around the country, available on the Internet at http://cirrus.sprl.umich.edu/wxnet/wxcam.html. If Internet access is unavailable, the activity can be done using the cloud chart in the classroom and pocket-size cloud charts that can be handed out to each student.

ADAPTATIONS FOR HIGH AND LOW ACHIEVERS

High Achievers: Encourage these students to do the Extensions and Follow-up Activities.

Low Achievers: Review the various types of clouds. Ask the students to identify clouds according to their shapes alone (e.g., just *cumulus* rather than *altocumulus*).

SCORING RUBRIC

Full credit should be given to students who complete their cloud diaries and have tried to identify each cloud they observed. It is not necessary that each identification be exact; sometimes real cloud types are difficult to identify precisely. Extra credit should be given to students who complete the Extension or Follow-up activities. The quiz can be scored from 1 to 4 correct.

 INTERNET TIE-INS   http://inspire.ospi.wednet.edu:8001/curric/weather/graphing/clouds.html
http://ww2010.atmos.uiuc.edu/(Gh)/guides/mtr/cld/cldtyp/home.rxml
http://www.nott.ac.uk/~ppyjdnmb/atmosphere/pages/cloudsgcse.html
http://australiansevereweather.simplenet.com/photography/

 **QUIZ**
1. List three ways in which air can be made to rise and form clouds.
2. List the three main cloud shapes.
3. What name would you give to a high, layered cloud?
4. True or False: A cloud is always a sign that it will soon rain.

Name _____   Date _____

Cloud Types

 BEFORE YOU BEGIN

Clouds appear in the sky almost every day. At any one time, about half of the entire globe is covered by clouds. But what is a cloud? A **cloud** is a visible mass made of water droplets (or, if it's cold enough, ice particles) that have condensed from the water vapor in the atmosphere. Water vapor requires a surface on which to condense. Small particles in the atmosphere provide such a surface. These particles, called **condensation nuclei**, are always present in some amounts in the atmosphere, and can be made of dust, ice, smoke, or even salt.

How do clouds form? They form when air lifts to a higher altitude. Parcels of air can be lifted to higher altitudes in several ways. One way is by **convection**. Convection occurs as warm, less-dense air rises, and cool, denser air sinks. Air can also be lifted as two weather fronts converge. And, air rises as it flows over mountaintops. Regardless of the cause, when the air rises, it cools. As a result, it can hold less water vapor than it did when it was warmer. The water vapor then condenses into water droplets or ice crystals, and a cloud forms. If the droplets or ice crystals grow large and heavy enough, they will fall from the cloud as **precipitation**.

The three main shapes of clouds are **stratus** (meaning "layered"), **cumulus** (meaning "heaped"), and **cirrus** (meaning "like a feathery lock of hair"). Stratus clouds cover large areas and give the sky a gray appearance. They are usually low-hanging clouds and signal that it is about to rain. Cumulus clouds are puffy, well-formed "cotton-ball" clouds seen at low to medium altitudes. They usually accompany fair weather. Cirrus clouds are high, wispy clouds that are almost always made of ice crystals rather than water droplets because of their altitude. Cirrus clouds may signal rain or snow within a few days. Most of the clouds we see are combinations of these shapes.

Clouds can also be classified more precisely according to their height in the sky. Low clouds with heights less than 2 km are given the prefix *strato-*. Medium-height clouds with heights between 2 km and 6 km have the prefix *alto-*. High-altitude clouds with heights ranging from 6 km to 12 km have the prefix *cirro-*. So a mid-level stratus cloud would be called "altostratus," a low cumulus cloud would be "stratocumulus," and a high-level stratus would be called "cirrostratus." There are other kinds of clouds that do not fit into this simple system, such as **nimbus** clouds, which contain rain. *Cumulonimbus* clouds, or thunderheads, are often seen in summer. They warn of approaching thunderstorms.

 MATERIALS

- Drawing paper and pencil
- Access to Internet sites for more examples of cloud types and descriptions
- Individual-size cloud chart, if available; otherwise, textbook showing cloud types

 **PROCEDURE**

1. Pick an outdoor spot at home or at school from which to observe clouds. Choose a site that allows you to observe as much of the sky as possible. You do not have to observe at the same time every day, but you should observe once each day for at least five days.

(continued)

       Walch Hands-on Science Series: Atmosphere and Weather

Cloud Types *(continued)*

2. Each time you observe, look for clouds. There may be few or many clouds visible, and there may be more than a single type. On a separate sheet of paper for each day, sketch each kind of cloud that you see. Use a cloud chart or textbook to help you identify the clouds you see. Also write down the general weather conditions. For example, is it sunny? Is it raining? Is it snowing? Be creative in the charts you make to record and analyze your data.

    If you are observing outdoors, do not stay outdoors if you see or hear   an approaching thunderstorm. Never look directly at the sun.

3. Repeat step 2 for at least five consecutive days.
4. Combine all of your observation sheets to create your "cloud diary."
5. If available, access the cloud-related Internet Web sites that your teacher gives you and examine images of the different types of clouds. Use data from these sites to verify the identify of the clouds you have sketched in your cloud diary.

DATA COLLECTION AND ANALYSIS

Cloud sketches, identifications, and general weather conditions should be written on the sheets that make up your cloud diary.

CONCLUDING QUESTIONS

1. Compare the kinds of weather usually associated with the different cloud types with your own observations of the clouds and weather at your location. Do they agree? _____
2. Why are condensation nuclei important in forming clouds? _____
   _____
3. What kind of cloud is least likely to be associated with precipitation? _____

   • **EXTENSION** There are types of clouds that do not fit into the simple classification schemes described earlier. Research these kinds of clouds (either on the Web sites you have visited or in books).
   • **EXTENSION** A typical cumulus cloud might contain 300,000 kg of water. If a liter of water weighs about 1 kg, how many liters of water are contained in the cloud? If a typical backyard swimming pool holds about 8,000 liters of water, how many pools could be filled with the water from a single cumulus cloud?

🌩 FOLLOW-UP ACTIVITIES 🌩

1. Research the mechanisms for lifting air and forming clouds.
2. Continue observing clouds for several more days. Based on your observations and what you have learned about clouds and associated weather, predict the weather for each successive day. Evaluate your success. What other data might have helped you improve your predictions?
3. Write and illustrate a book for small children that explains how clouds form and explains the different types of clouds.

The Water Cycle: What a Trip!

 INSTRUCTIONAL OBJECTIVES

Students will be able to

- describe and demonstrate how the water cycle works.

 NATIONAL SCIENCE STANDARDS ADDRESSED

Students demonstrate an understanding of

- energy in the earth's system.
- conservation of matter.
- the concepts of change and constancy, cause and effect.

Students demonstrate scientific inquiry and problem-solving skills by

- identifying and controlling variables.
- using relevant concepts to explain data.

Students demonstrate effective scientific communication by

- representing data in multiple ways.
- arguing from evidence and data.

 MATERIALS

- Medium-size frying pan
- Pyrex™ or other heat-proof measuring cup, preferably 2-cup size
- Glass or stoneware dinner plate about as wide as the frying pan
- Ice cubes
- Gas or electric burner

 Safety icon

 INTERNET TIE-INS   http://ww2010.atmos.uiuc.edu/(6h)/guides/mtr/hyd/home.rxml
http://publish.uwrl.usu.edu/h20cycle1.html

 QUIZ
1. What do we mean by the "water cycle"?
2. Where does most of the water in the atmosphere come from?
3. True or False: Transpiration moves water from the land to the atmosphere.
4. Define "runoff."
5. Where does precipitation take water from, and where does it deliver the water?

HELPFUL HINTS AND DISCUSSION

Time frame: About 30 minutes
Structure: Individuals
Location: At home

In this activity, students will simulate the water cycle at home. It is important that the materials used be heat-proof, and that the exercise be done **with adult supervision**. The function of the measuring cup is to provide a platform to suspend the dinner plate above the boiling water, so it should be sufficiently wide to keep the ice cube-covered dinner plate stable, but not so wide as to cover most of the underside (condensing surface) of the dinner plate.

ADAPTATIONS FOR HIGH AND LOW ACHIEVERS

High Achievers: Encourage these students to do the Extensions and Follow-up activities.

Low Achievers: Review the relevant concepts of evaporation and condensation before assigning this activity.

SCORING RUBRIC

Full credit should be given to students who describe their results in complete sentences. Students should observe the drops of water drip from the underside of the plate into the frying pan. Extra credit should be given to students who complete the Extension or Follow-up activities. The quiz can be scored from 1 to 5 correct.

Name _____   Date _____

The Water Cycle: What a Trip!

 BEFORE YOU BEGIN

Water is necessary to sustain all life on Earth. Where is all the earth's water? In the oceans? In the polar icecaps? In the atmosphere? In the ground? In living things? Yes, Earth's water is distributed among all of these places. But, water doesn't stay permanently in any one place. For example, you have seen rain, you have noticed water droplets condense on a cold glass, and you have experienced evaporation of water from your skin. In all of these situations, water is merely moving from one place or one form to another. It is not being created or destroyed. The total amount of water on Earth stays very nearly constant, with a volume equal to about 1.2 billion cubic kilometers. The circulation of water among the earth's oceans, land, atmosphere, and living things is a continuous process called the **water cycle.**

The main processes of the water cycle are:
- **evaporation** from the oceans to the atmosphere
- **transpiraton** from plants to the atmosphere
- **precipitation** from the atmosphere to the land and oceans
- **runoff** from the land to the oceans

Most of the water vapor in the atmosphere comes from evaporation from the oceans. Transpiration from plants also produces water vapor, as does breathing by animals. Water vapor condenses as the moist air rises and cools, forming clouds. Air movement transports clouds until they release their water through precipitation. Precipitation falling on the land can flow into lakes, rivers, and streams, and eventually into the ocean as runoff—and then the cycle starts again. Some precipitation evaporates back into the atmosphere directly, or it can be absorbed into the ground as groundwater, which trickles into rivers and streams, and back into the oceans. In this activity, you will simulate the water cycle in your kitchen!

 MATERIALS

- Medium-size frying pan
- Pyrex™ or other heat-proof measuring cup, preferably 2-cup size
- Glass or stoneware dinner plate about as wide as the frying pan
- Ice cubes
- Gas or electric burner

 Safety icon

 PROCEDURE

Be sure to have adult supervision when performing this activity.

1. Fill a frying pan with about 1 cm of water and place it on an unlit burner.

2. Invert the measuring cup and place it in the center of the frying pan. If the measuring cup tries to float, let some of the trapped air out of it by tipping the spout up.

3. Place the dinner plate on top of the inverted measuring cup, keeping it as stable as possible and approximately centered. Don't worry if the plate tilts a little bit to one side.   *(continued)*

The Water Cycle: What a Trip! *(continued)*

4. Cover the plate with ice cubes. Don't worry if the ice cubes slide toward one side of the plate. The important thing is to make sure that the plate remains stable.

5. Turn the burner on medium and wait for the water to boil. When it starts to boil, turn the burner to low.

6. Watch the underside of the plate. If the plate is tilted, pay special attention to the downward side of the plate.

7. Observe for several minutes and record what you see. *Do not* let all the water evaporate from the pan—add a little cold water if necessary to keep the bottom of the frying pan covered during the activity.

8. Turn off the burner and wait at least 30 minutes before dismantling the setup.

DATA COLLECTION AND ANALYSIS

1. On a separate sheet of paper, describe and explain your observations of the underside of the plate.

2. Draw a diagram of your experimental setup and label the relevant parts.

3. Draw a diagram of the real water cycle and label the relevant parts.

CONCLUDING QUESTIONS

1. Relate the water in the frying pan, the ice cube-covered plate, and the drops of water falling from the underside of the plate to elements in the real water cycle.

    _____

    _____

    _____

2. How could you have sped up the process in your experiment? _____

    _____

    _____

3. On a separate sheet (or sheets) of paper, write and illustrate a short story from the point of view of a drop of water in the ocean. Describe your drop's adventures through the water cycle.

(continued)

Name _____   Date _____

The Water Cycle: What a Trip! *(continued)*

 EXTENSION Some of the water vapor in the experiment escaped around the sides of the plate without condensing. If you left the burner on for long enough, all the water in the frying pan would be gone. Would this happen in the real water cycle? Why or why not?

🌩 **FOLLOW-UP ACTIVITIES** 🌩

1. Sometimes the water cycle is locally out of balance—too much precipitation can cause flooding, too little can cause a drought. Research your local area's weather history and see if there has been a flood or a drought in the past. How did the flood or drought affect the people in your area?

2. You can demonstrate transpiration by sealing a small potted plant in a plastic bag. Place the plant in the light, and observe the inside of the bag. What do you see, and where did it come from? You can also show that *you* produce water vapor by breathing onto a small mirror. What do you see?

INSTRUCTIONAL OBJECTIVES

Students will be able to

- explain what lightning is.
- demonstrate an electrical discharge.
- explain what a capacitor is.

NATIONAL SCIENCE STANDARDS ADDRESSED

Students demonstrate an understanding of

- energy in the earth's system.
- the structure and properties of matter.
- electrical forces.
- interaction of energy and matter.

Students demonstrate scientific inquiry and problem-solving skills by

- identifying and controlling variables.
- using relevant concepts to explain observed phenomena.

Students demonstrate effective scientific communication by

- arguing from evidence.

MATERIALS

- Aluminum foil
- Plastic food wrap
- Balloon
- Textbook or telephone book (a paperback is too small)
- Paper clip
- Plastic, glass, or earthenware bowl
- Scissors (optional)
- Radio (for follow-up activity)
- Metric ruler

 Safety icon

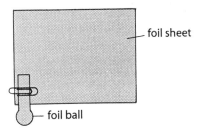

foil sheet

foil ball

HELPFUL HINTS AND DISCUSSION

Time frame: About 50 minutes
Structure: Individuals
Location: At home

In this activity, students will create a miniature lightning bolt. This exercise can fail if the materials and conditions are not right. In particular, the capacitor cannot be charged if the insulator between the aluminum foil pieces is even slightly conductive, if there is a slightly conductive path from the capacitor to the table or counter, or if the ambient humidity is very high.

Students may need to experiment to get a functioning capacitor and charge it enough to create a spark—encourage them to try variations until they succeed. They can vary the sizes and shapes of the conducting aluminum foil pieces, the type and thickness of the insulating layer (not all plastic food wraps are created equal), the means of insulating the book from the table, etc. In this way they may find that paper—and by implication, its parent material, wood—are not as good an electrical insulator as they may have thought. This can be related to what could happen if you stand under a tree during a lightning storm. This activity is an excellent opportunity for students to exercise their imaginations.

While this activity is absolutely safe for the students, static discharges can damage some electronic equipment. Be sure students keep their homemade capacitors away from computers, electronic games, etc.

ADAPTATIONS FOR HIGH AND LOW ACHIEVERS

High Achievers: Encourage every student to try the Extension. High achievers should be encouraged to do the Follow-up activities.

Low Achievers: Encourage every student to try the Extension with the help of the high achievers.

Side view

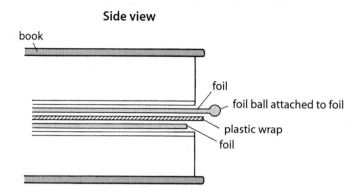

 **INTERNET TIE-INS**   http://www.richmond.edu/~ed344/97/wildweather/lightning1.html
http://www.dir.ucar.edu/esig/socasp/lightning.html

 QUIZ   1. What is lightning?
2. How do clouds become charged?
3. What does a capacitor do?
4. Describe an example of static electricity other than lightning.

Name _____   Date _____

Lightning!

BEFORE YOU BEGIN

Thunderstorms can be beautiful and frightening at the same time. Of the heavy rain, strong winds, thunder, and lightning that make up a thunderstorm, **lightning** is the most dangerous. About 100 people are struck by lightning every year in the United States. Lightning is an extreme example of a static electrical discharge, or spark, created when an object with a stored electrical charge finds a conducting path across which its charge can flow. Electrical charges can be positive or negative. **Opposite** charges attract, while **like** charges repel each other. When you get a shock from touching a metal doorknob after walking across a carpet in your socks, you experience a static electrical discharge. You picked up excess negative electrical charge as your feet rubbed across the carpet. The excess charge was stored in your body until the doorknob provided a path for it to flow from you.

In a thunderstorm, the object storing electrical charge is a cloud. The charge is created by water droplets or ice particles rubbing against each other and the air as they move around in the cloud—just as you become charged as your feet move across a carpet.

There are artificial devices called **capacitors**, which store electrical charge. These are used in many electronic products such as radios, microwave ovens, and automobile ignition systems. A thunderstorm acts as a huge natural capacitor, capable of storing an enormous charge. Any capacitor, whether natural or artificial, consists of two conducting objects separated by an insulating (nonconducting) substance. In a thunderstorm, the conductors are moist clouds or the ground. Air does not easily conduct electricity and thus serves as an insulator. The discharge can flow from cloud to cloud, or between a cloud and the ground (as it flows between you and a doorknob). Discharge occurs when the stored charge becomes too great for the insulator (air) to hold back.

In this activity, you will create a miniature lightning bolt by building, charging, and discharging a capacitor. You will create the charge in the same way that a thunderstorm does—by rubbing. The spark you create cannot harm you, but it does nonetheless demonstrate the potential power of lightning.

 ## MATERIALS

- Aluminum foil
- Plastic food wrap
- Balloon
- Textbook or telephone book (a paperback is too small)

- Paper clip
- Plastic, glass, or earthenware bowl
- Scissors (optional)
- Radio (for follow-up activity)
- Metric ruler

 ## PROCEDURE

Static discharges can damage some electronic equipment. Be sure to keep your homemade capacitor away from computers, electronic games, etc.

1. Cut or tear two rectangular pieces of aluminum foil, each a centimeter or so smaller than a page in the book you are using for this experiment. Try to keep the foil from getting crumpled.

(continued)

Lightning! *(continued)*

2. Cut or tear a rectangular piece of plastic food wrap a few centimeters larger than a page in the book. Try to keep the plastic wrap from sticking to itself.

3. Cut or tear another strip of aluminum foil about 2 cm wide and 10 cm long. Crumple one end into a ball, leaving the other end flat. Using the paper clip, attach the flat end of the strip to one of the two pieces of aluminum foil you cut earlier, as shown in the diagram to the right.

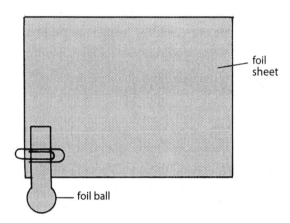

foil sheet

foil ball

4. You will now make an aluminum sandwich. Open your book somewhere near the middle. Place one piece of aluminum foil on the page, centered so that no foil extends near or past the edges of the page. Now put the plastic wrap over the page so that it completely covers the foil and extends past the edges of the page. Place the piece of foil with the foil ball attached on top of the plastic, directly over the first piece of foil. Be sure that the ball of aluminum foil extends past the edge of the page. Close the book. (See the diagram below.)

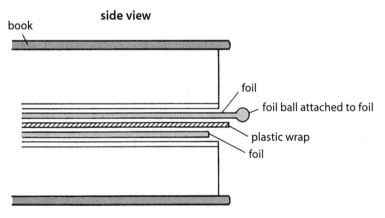

side view

book

foil

foil ball attached to foil

plastic wrap

foil

5. Place the book on a table or counter, using a glass, plastic, or earthenware bowl to elevate the book a few centimeters off the surface.

6. Inflate the balloon and tie it off.

7. Put one hand in your pocket or at your side (this is to keep you insulated from the table or counter). Rub the balloon vigorously on your hair for 5 to 10 seconds. Then touch the balloon to the aluminum foil ball, rolling the balloon so that a lot of its surface comes in contact with the foil. You may hear a slight crackling sound as you do this. Repeat twice more.

(continued)

Lightning! *(continued)*

8. Without touching anything, set the balloon aside and move your finger to touch the foil ball. Observe what happens. Darken the room as much as you can, and repeat steps 7 and 8.

If the exercise is successful, you will have made a safe, miniature lightning bolt, in much the way nature does.

EXTENSION Whether your exercise succeeds or fails to work, many variations can be tried. As long as you have two pieces of a conductor separated by an insulator, you have a capacitor. Try pieces of aluminum foil of different sizes and shapes. Try different insulators, including various papers and plastics in several thicknesses. Also, try different ways of forming and supporting the whole apparatus. If possible, try this exercise under both humid and dry conditions. Record your results.

DATA COLLECTION AND ANALYSIS

1. What happened when you brought your finger near the aluminum foil ball? _____

_____

2. With what senses did you perceive this? Do you perceive lightning with the same senses? What do we call the audible effect of lightning? _____

_____

_____

CONCLUDING QUESTIONS

1. If you had trouble making the experiment work, or if you tried variations of the exercise, which changes helped you to create a spark, and which didn't?

_____

_____

_____

2. Most types of paper are actually slightly conductive. Many people stand under trees for protection in a thunderstorm. Knowing what most paper is made from, do you think this is a good idea? Explain your answer.

_____

_____

3. Describe what happened to your hair when you rubbed the balloon on it. Research why this happens.

_____

_____

Lightning! *(continued)*

 FOLLOW-UP ACTIVITIES

1. List as many examples of static electricity in everyday life as you can think of. Remember that when substances rub against each other, they can become charged, and then discharge with a spark that you can see and/or feel. In addition, oppositely charged substances will attract and sometimes cling to each other.

2. Listening to the radio on a summer evening, you may have noticed some clicking and popping sounds interfering with the music. These bursts are usually caused by lightning discharges—sometimes nearby, but often from many kilometers or even hundreds of kilometers away. To simulate this, turn on a radio and set it on the AM band, if possible. Take the balloon you used in this activity, and charge it up as before. Bring it in contact with the radio, just as you brought it in contact with the aluminum foil ball. Note what happens.

Violent Storms: Tornadoes and Hurricanes

 INSTRUCTIONAL OBJECTIVES

Students will be able to

- explain the development of tornadoes and hurricanes.
- describe how these storms can inflict significant property damage.

 NATIONAL SCIENCE STANDARDS ADDRESSED

Students demonstrate an understanding of

- energy in the earth's system.
- effects of heat and pressure.
- the concept of cause and effect.

Students demonstrate scientific inquiry and problem-solving skills by

- identifying and controlling variables (extension).
- working individually and in teams to collect and share information and ideas.

Students demonstrate effective scientific communication by

- arguing from evidence and data.

MATERIALS

For each pair:

PART A

- Two empty plastic 2-liter clear (uncolored) soda bottles
- Duct tape or vinyl electrical tape
- Food coloring
- Water

PART B

- One 2-liter soda bottle, empty and very clean

PART C

- Large tray or roasting pan with sides
- Sand
- Electric hair dryer
- Ice cream sticks or tongue depressors
- Water
- Cardboard sheet (optional)
- One or two sheets of paper and pencil for sketching

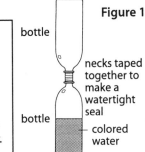

Figure 1

bottle

necks taped together to make a watertight seal

bottle

colored water

HELPFUL HINTS AND DISCUSSION

Time frame: 40 minutes, or one class period
Structure: Part A and C: pairs; Part B: individuals
Location: In class

One member of each pair should do the setup for Part A, and the other member should do the setup and assembly for Part C. Pairs should then do Parts A and C together, with each student recording his or her own observations separately. Part B is an individual exercise.

ADAPTATIONS FOR HIGH AND LOW ACHIEVERS

High Achievers: Encourage these students to do the Extension and Follow-up activities.

Low Achievers: Pair these students with high achievers for Parts A and C.

SCORING RUBRIC

Full credit should be given to students who record full and reasonable observations for each of the three parts, and who make reasonable "before" and "after" sketches for Part C. Extra credit can be given to students who complete the Extension or Follow-up activities. The quiz can be scored from 1 to 5 correct.

 INTERNET TIE-INS   http://ncstormtrack.com/guide/sites.html
http://www.meteor.wisc.edu/~hopkins/aos100/twister.htm

QUIZ
1. How are tornadoes related to thunderstorms?
2. True or False: The air pressure inside a tornado is much higher than normal atmospheric pressure.
3. What is a storm surge?
4. Give two other names for hurricanes.
5. What is a vortex?

Figure 2   Side view of roasting pan

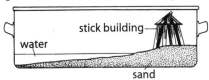

stick building

water

sand

Name _____ Date _____

Violent Storms: Tornadoes and Hurricanes

 BEFORE YOU BEGIN

You may have seen them on TV—men and women who track down and photograph some of the most violent storms on the planet. They are *storm chasers*, who put themselves in danger to record tornadoes, the fascinating but deadly offspring of violent thunderstorms. Hurricanes are much larger and long-lived storms than tornadoes, but they share several properties with tornadoes besides their danger.

Tornadoes are formed when a rotating inward flow of air, or **vortex**, forms around a rapidly rising column of air within a thunderstorm. As the upward speed increases, the air pressure drops, and the vortex shrinks in diameter. The spinning air speeds up in the same way as a spinning figure skater spins faster by bringing her arms in close to her sides. In this way, very high winds are born inside a tornado. These high winds, as well as the very low atmospheric pressure inside the funnel (as much as 20 percent below normal atmospheric pressure), produce the incredible damage tornadoes are capable of.

Hurricanes, which are much larger storm systems, are actually intense low-pressure regions of their own. They are extreme examples of **tropical storms**, which, as their name implies, originate over warm, tropical ocean waters. A hurricane starts as a mild low-pressure region far from a warm front or cold front. It intensifies as heat, upward air motion, and wind speeds increase. While hurricane winds are not as fast as winds in tornadoes (though tornadoes are sometimes spun off by hurricanes), they cover a much greater area. Hurricanes can also push ahead a **storm surge** of ocean water, flooding low-lying coastal areas. In some parts of the world, hurricanes are called **typhoons** or **cyclones**.

MATERIALS

PART A

- Two empty plastic 2-liter clear (uncolored) soda bottles
- Duct tape or vinyl electrical tape
- Food coloring
- Water

PART B

- One 2-liter soda bottle, empty and very clean

PART C

- Large tray or roasting pan with sides
- Sand
- Electric hair dryer
- Ice cream sticks or tongue depressors
- Water
- Cardboard sheet (optional)
- One or two sheets of paper and pencil for sketching

PROCEDURE

PART A

1. Tear the labels off the two soda bottles so you can see through them.

2. Fill one bottle about halfway with water. Add 5 to 10 drops of food coloring.

3. Place the opening of the second bottle against the opening of the first bottle, and tape them together securely as shown in Figure 1 on the next page. Be sure the connection is watertight.

(continued)

Violent Storms: Tornadoes and Hurricanes (continued)

4. Grab the connected necks of the bottles with one hand, and place the other hand below the bottom bottle to hold it securely. Moving both hands together with a swirling motion, get the water in the bottle spinning as fast as you can.

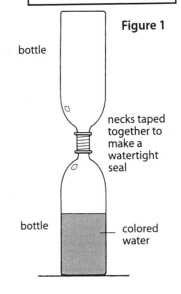

Figure 1

bottle

necks taped together to make a watertight seal

bottle

colored water

5. Quickly flip the pair of bottles end-over-end, and hold the originally empty bottle steady on a counter or tabletop. You should see a tornado-like vortex as the water empties from the top bottle into the bottom. Observe what happens, and record your observations in the Data Collection and Analysis section. Pay particular attention to the speed of rotation of the water near the center of the vortex compared with the speed near the wall of the bottle.

PART B

1. Put the opening of the clean soda bottle in your mouth and suck in as hard as you can. Observe what happens, and record your observations in the Data Collection and Analysis section.

PART C

1. Build a beachfront community inside a roasting pan. Fill the pan with sand as shown in the figure below, making sure that the surface of the sand slopes downward toward one side of the pan. Add enough water to make a shoreline, so that about $\frac{1}{3}$ of the sand is still above the water, representing "land." The other $\frac{2}{3}$ of the pan is "ocean." Build two or three crude structures out of the ice cream sticks on the sand near the waterline (build cheap—don't use glue or fasteners of any kind).

Side view of roasting pan

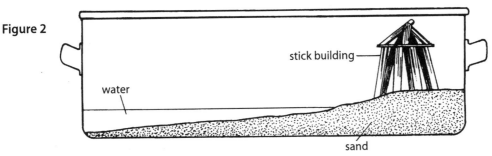

Figure 2

water

stick building

sand

2. Make a "before" sketch of your community.

3. Holding the hair dryer away from the roasting pan, turn it on high fan, low heat. Blow air onto the water in the pan so that the water piles up on the "shore" in waves. Try not to blow air directly on the structures you built. Use a cardboard sheet to block the direct wind from the structures, if necessary. Push the water onto the "shore" repeatedly so that the action of the water causes some of the sand to wash away. Observe what happens, and record your observations in the Data Collection and Analysis section.

4. Make an "after" sketch of your community.

(continued)

Violent Storms: Tornadoes and Hurricanes *(continued)*

 EXTENSION Using the materials you have available, design different beachfront structures. Try varying the kind of base and support for the structures. Repeat Part C, step 3, for each kind of structure. Compare the effects of the storm surge on all of them. Can you draw any conclusions about the kinds of structures that are most resistant to beach erosion?

 DATA COLLECTION AND ANALYSIS

PART A: Describe what you observed in Part A, step 5. Pay special attention to the speed of the water near the center of the vortex compared with the speed of the water near the wall of the bottle.

_____

_____

PART B: Describe what happened when you sucked in on the bottle.

_____

PART C: Describe what happened in Part C, step 3, when the hair dryer blew water onto the "shore." Compare the "before" and "after" sketches of your beachfront community.

_____

CONCLUDING QUESTIONS

1. In what way is the vortex in Part A similar to a tornado?

_____

2. Does the water in the center of the vortex rotate faster or slower than the water near the edge?

_____

3. How does the vortex in Part A differ from real weather vortices (plural of *vortex*) such as tornadoes and hurricanes?

_____

4. Describe a way, other than the direct effect of wind, in which hurricanes can produce property damage. How do your observations support this?

_____

_____

 FOLLOW-UP ACTIVITIES

1. In ordinary life we encounter many small, often short-lived, vortices. Now that you know what to look for, try to recall similar phenomena and make a list of them. To help you get started, think about some of the following: taking a bath, rowing a boat, stirring a glass of soda, getting caught in a wind gust in a dusty or snowy area.
2. Tornadoes and hurricanes are dangerous. Research and write a brief report on the recommended precautions for keeping safe in such storms. Describe the places in the world and in the United States where tornadoes and hurricanes are most common.

The Reasons for the Seasons

 INSTRUCTIONAL OBJECTIVES

Students will be able to

- explain the existence of seasons on the earth.
- create models to demonstrate the reasons for the seasons.

 NATIONAL SCIENCE STANDARDS ADDRESSED

Students demonstrate an understanding of

- transfer of energy.
- energy in the earth's system.
- the sun as a source of energy.
- the concept of cause and effect.

Students demonstrate scientific inquiry and problem-solving skills by

- framing questions and identifying variables.
- working individually and in teams to collect information and share ideas.

Students demonstrate effective scientific communication by

- arguing from evidence and data.
- explaining a scientific concept to other students.

 MATERIALS

- Flashlight
- Pencil
- Clear desk or table area about 1 meter square
- 8.5" × 11" sheet of plain paper
- Ruler with centimeter and millimeter divisions
- Clear tape
- Marker

HELPFUL HINTS AND DISCUSSION

Time frame: 40 minutes, or one class period
Structure: Pairs
Location: In class

In this activity, students will simulate how the sun's rays hit the earth at different seasons in different parts of the world. Typical flashlights create several concentric beams of varying brightness, and the students may have difficulty deciding which beam to concentrate on. That is why the students begin with the flashlight flat on the paper, rather than aiming at the paper while holding the flashlight from above. In step 3, the lit shape should be an ellipse, which looks like a flattened circle. Make sure that the students tilt the flashlight onto the back edge of its rim, keeping it in contact with both the pencil and the paper. Instruct them not to lift the flashlight off the paper. Remind the students that the concentration of sunlight is *inversely proportional* to the total area illuminated. So a square centimeter, say, of a larger illuminated ellipse receives less sunlight than that same area of a smaller illuminated ellipse.

Figure 1: The Tilt of the Earth's Axis Relative to the Sun at Each Season

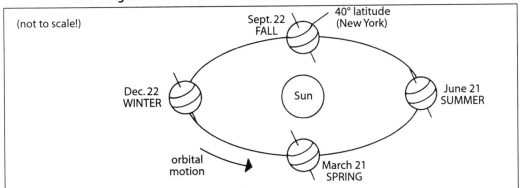

Figure 2: The Angle of Incoming Sunlight During Summer and Winter for Northern and Southern Hemispheres

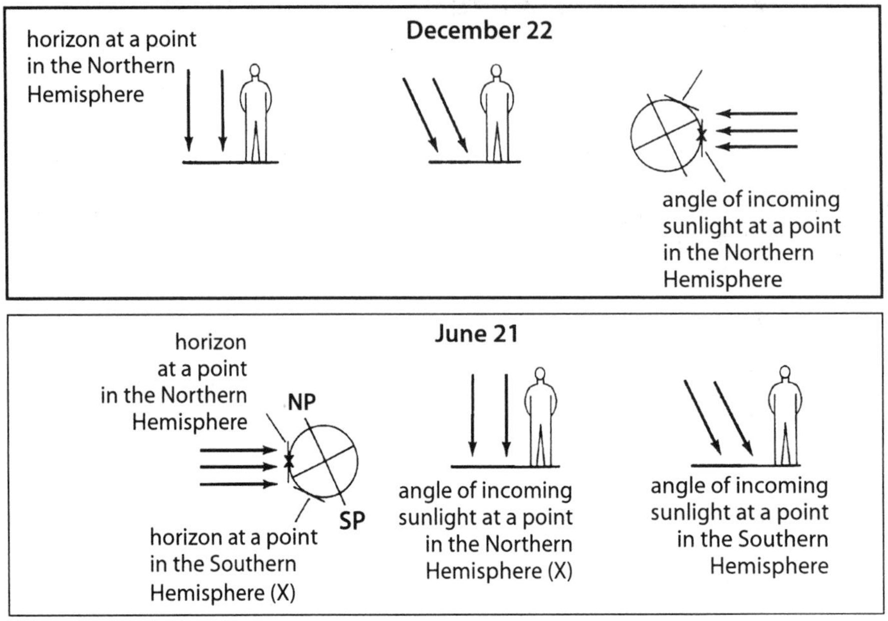

December 22

horizon at a point in the Northern Hemisphere

angle of incoming sunlight at a point in the Northern Hemisphere

June 21

horizon at a point in the Northern Hemisphere

NP

SP

horizon at a point in the Southern Hemisphere (X)

angle of incoming sunlight at a point in the Northern Hemisphere (X)

angle of incoming sunlight at a point in the Southern Hemisphere

ADAPTATIONS FOR HIGH AND LOW ACHIEVERS

High Achievers: In step 3, high achievers can calculate the relative areas of ellipses created by tilting the flashlight at different angles. Using a protractor, these students can hold the flashlight to simulate the angle of sunlight on the first day of winter and of summer at their latitude. Measured from the vertical, these angles are (latitude + 23.5 degrees) and (latitude – 23.5 degrees), respectively. Have the students calculate the ratio of the areas of the two ellipses created in this way, thereby estimating the relative solar energy received on those dates at their latitude. More energy is received per unit area when the ellipse is smaller.

Low Achievers: Review the relevant concepts prior to the experiment, including how to measure the area of a circle and an ellipse, and the definition of latitude. These students should be encouraged to do the Extension and Follow-up activities.

SCORING RUBRIC

Full credit should be given to students who answer the Concluding Questions correctly. Extra credit should be given to students who do the Extension or a Follow-up activity. The quiz can be scored from 1 to 4 correct.

 **INTERNET TIE-IN**   http://www.nmstc.ca/nmst/educ/ideabank/astroprg/probing/Bkground/eseason.htm

QUIZ
1. On what date does Northern Hemisphere summer begin?
2. What effect does the angle of incoming sunlight have on heating any particular spot on Earth?
3. Why isn't it hottest on June 21 and coldest on December 22 in the Northern Hemisphere?
4. Is the height of the noontime sun highest or lowest on December 22 in the Southern Hemisphere?

The Reasons for the Seasons

 BEFORE YOU BEGIN

If you live anywhere in the continental United States, you have experienced the parade of the seasons. In most parts of the world, seasons are distinguished by changes in the average temperature. Winter is coldest (cold enough for sledding and snowball fights in some areas), and summer is warmest. Spring and autumn are in between. Since the surface of the earth gets nearly all of its heat from the sunlight that falls on it, you might correctly expect that the seasons are caused by changes in the amount of solar energy that an area receives at different times of year.

You may have noticed that the noontime sun appears higher in the sky in summer than in winter. This is because the earth's equator is tilted relative to the plane of the earth's orbit around the sun, as shown in Figure 1. At different times of year at a particular latitude, the light (and therefore heat) of the sun is more overhead than at other times.

If the sun's light arrives at a low angle (far from overhead), then the light is spread out over a larger area than if it arrives close to overhead (see Figure 2). Less energy falls on each portion of the ground, and the season will be a cold one. But if the sun is close to overhead, then its light will be concentrated into a smaller area. More energy falls on each portion of the ground, and the season will be warm. Actually, the coldest and warmest times of year do not occur at exactly the times of highest and lowest noontime sun, but are delayed a month or so because the land, water, and air take time to heat up and cool down.

As shown in Figure 1, New York City has a latitude of about 40° N. At noon on June 21 in New York, the sun is more nearly overhead than it is at noon on December 22. The sunlight on June 21 is therefore more direct and more concentrated than it is on December 22. At noon on March 21 and September 22, the sunlight is less concentrated than on June 21, but more concentrated than on December 22.

Figure 1: The Tilt of the Earth's Axis Relative to the Sun at Each Season

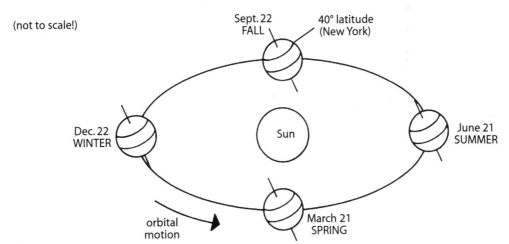

(continued)

The Reasons for the Seasons

 MATERIALS

- Flashlight
- Pencil
- Clear desk or table area about 1 meter square
- 8.5" × 11" sheet of plain paper

- Ruler with centimeter and millimeter divisions
- Clear tape
- Marker

Figure 2: The Angle of Incoming Sunlight During Summer and Winter for Northern and Southern Hemispheres

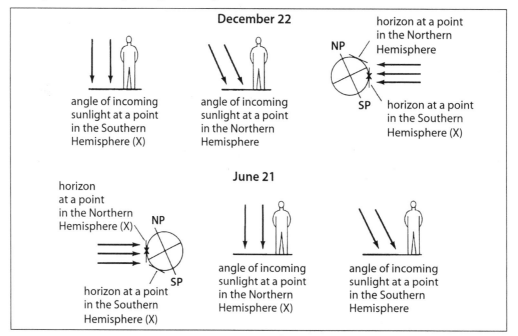

PROCEDURE

1. Darken the room. Tape the paper down on the table. Turn on the flashlight. Have one member of your group hold the flashlight, lit end down, flat on the paper. The other group member should trace around the rim of the flashlight.

2. Draw in the diameter, D, of the circle you just traced. Measure it in centimeters, and enter this value in the Data Collection and Analysis section. Calculate the area of the circle using the formula $A = \pi D^2/4$ and enter this value.

3. Now switch tasks with your partner. Holding the lit flashlight against the paper with one hand, hold the pencil flat on the table with the other hand. Tilting the flashlight back on its rim, slide the pencil halfway under the rim of the flashlight. Hold the flashlight against the pencil so that the angle of tilt stays the same. Always keep the back of the flashlight rim in contact with the table. The group member not holding the flashlight and pencil should now trace the resulting lit area on the paper. There may be several different brightness levels in the lit area, especially at the center. Just concentrate on and trace the largest lit area (see Figure 3).

(continued)

Name _____ Date _____

Figure 3

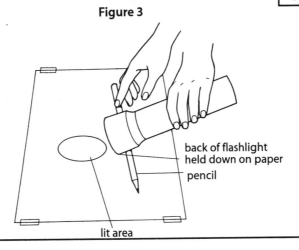

back of flashlight
held down on paper
pencil

lit area

4. Measure the longest dimension (L) of the lit shape and record it in the Data Collection and Analysis section. Measure the shortest dimension (S) and record it as well.

5. Calculate the area of the geometric figure using the formula $A = \pi LS/4$ and record it.

6. Calculate the ratio of the area of the figure from step 3 to the area of the circle and record it.

DATA COLLECTION AND ANALYSIS

Diameter of flashlight rim in step 2: _____cm

Area of circle in step 2: _____cm^2

What is the geometrical shape of the area traced in step 3? _____

Longest dimension measured in step 4: L= _____cm

Shortest dimension measured in step 4: S= _____cm

Area of figure in step 4: _____cm^2

Ratio of figure area to circle area (figure area/circle area): _____

This ratio illustrates the difference in how spread out sunlight reaching the ground is in winter compared to how direct and concentrated it is in summer.

CONCLUDING QUESTIONS

1. Which season does the model you created in step 2 represent? _____

2. Which season does the model you created in step 3 represent? _____

3. Why is sunlight more spread out in winter than in summer? _____

   _____

4. What is the main reason why we have seasons on the earth? _____

   _____

(continued)

The Reasons for the Seasons *(continued)*

⇨ EXTENSIONS

1. The earth is actually a little closer to the sun in January (Northern Hemisphere winter) than in June (Northern Hemisphere summer). What effect might you expect this to have on the relative severity of winter and warmth of summer in the Northern and Southern hemispheres?

   _____

   _____

2. Research—in newspaper archives or an atlas—the values and dates of the highest and lowest average temperatures for your area. Do the same for several other interesting locations around the world, including one near the equator. Note which locations have the largest and smallest variations in average temperature over the course of a year. Why do you think this is so?

   _____

   _____

   _____

   _____

   _____

FOLLOW-UP ACTIVITIES

1. Using plastic foam or clay, make a model of the earth. Paint the equator on the earth, and stick a pencil or dowel through the center of the earth to represent its axis of rotation. Using a lightbulb as the sun, act out the earth's orbit with your model. As your Earth orbits, make sure to keep its axis always tilted about 23° to the plane of its orbital path and pointed always in the same direction as in Figure 1. Note how the illumination of any particular latitude changes over the course of a year.

2. Imagine that the earth's equator is in the same plane as its orbit around the sun. Therefore, there are no seasons on the earth. How would you feel about that? Write a poem about a world with no seasons.

Researching Climate and Climate Zones

✔ INSTRUCTIONAL OBJECTIVES

Students will be able to

- distinguish between weather and climate.
- describe climate zones.
- explain the effects of "climate makers."

🌐 NATIONAL SCIENCE STANDARDS ADDRESSED

Students demonstrate an understanding of

- energy in the earth's system.
- the concepts of change and constancy, cause and effect.

Students demonstrate scientific inquiry and problem-solving skills by

- proposing and considering alternative explanations.
- using evidence from reliable sources.
- acquiring information from multiple sources, including the Internet.

Students demonstrate effective scientific communication by

- arguing from evidence and data.

✂ MATERIALS

- Pen or pencil
- Access to a world atlas and an encyclopedia
- Internet access

HELPFUL HINTS AND DISCUSSION

Time frame: 40 minutes, possibly over several days
Structure: Individuals
Location: In class or at home

In this activity, students will research the climates of different areas around the world and draw conclusions about the factors that determine the climate of each area. In searching for the required information, students may find that sources sometimes refer to conditions at one or more airports near a city rather than the city itself. Assure students that it is acceptable to use this data. Review the vocabulary words with the class prior to beginning this activity.

ADAPTATIONS FOR HIGH AND LOW ACHIEVERS

High Achievers: These students should be encouraged to do the Extension and Follow-up activities. These students should extend their climate classifications to include more detail and more descriptive classifications, such as *marine, Mediterranean, continental,* etc. These classifications should be described in the climate chapter of most textbooks. The required data is available on the Internet at http://www.worldclimate.com/.

Low Achievers: Review all relevant concepts about climate zones and climate factors. Be sure to have sufficient reference material on hand during the exercise, and make assistance available for the Internet portion of the exercise.

SCORING RUBRIC

Full credit should be given to students who enter reasonable numbers in all parts of the data table. Consider the climate determinations correct if they are supported by the data collected. It may be difficult to decide if some locations are humid or semiarid, so accept either if there is doubt. Extra credit should be given to students who complete the Extension or Follow-up activities. The quiz can be scored from 1 to 5 correct.

💻 INTERNET TIE-INS

http://www.cdc.noaa.gov/~cas/climate.url.html
http://www.worldclimate.com/
http://www4.ncdc.noaa.gov/cgi-win/wwcgi.dll?wwnolos~Product~PB-016#TABLES

❓ QUIZ

1. How does climate differ from weather?
2. Write down the three latitude-based climate zones from coldest to hottest.
3. Write down the three precipitation-based climate types from wettest to driest.
4. Describe how a mountain range can be a climate maker.
5. True or False: You can reliably predict the climate of a place knowing only its latitude.

Name _____   Date _____

Researching Climate and Climate Zones

 BEFORE YOU BEGIN

What do you think of when someone mentions Antarctica? How about the Amazon River basin? You probably imagine frigid snowfields and dense jungle vegetation, in that order. You don't have to imagine any particular day—you just conjure up a mental image of the average weather conditions in each of these places. It's their *climate* you are imagining. **Climate** is **long-term average weather**, a general pattern of weather that repeats over many years.

Climates around the world are complex, resulting from both global and local effects. Climates can be roughly classified according to average temperature and average precipitation. The average temperature of a location is determined primarily by its **latitude**, or distance from the equator. Places near the equator get the most total sunlight averaged over the year and so are the warmest. Places near the poles get the least and are the coldest. The earth can thus be divided into climate **zones** according to latitude: the hot **tropical** zone straddling the equator, the cold **polar** zones around the North and South poles, and the **temperate** zones in between, where temperatures are generally less extreme. Most of the United States lies in the northern temperate zone.

The average precipitation of a place also depends to some extent on its latitude. Global circulation patterns in the atmosphere cause air to generally rise near the equator and near ±60° latitude, and sink near ±30° latitude and near the poles. When rising air reaches cooler levels of the atmosphere, moisture in it may condense into clouds, often producing precipitation. Conversely, sinking air tends to get warmer and drier, and precipitation is less likely. This is why jungles are found near the equator, while many of the world's deserts are near ±30° latitude. Places can be categorized by their precipitation as **arid**, **semiarid**, and **humid**, going from driest to wettest.

Of course, climate isn't that simple. Many local factors, called **climate makers**, can modify the climate you would expect from latitude alone. For example, a location near the middle of a continent tends to be drier than one near the ocean. Similarly, the side of a mountain range facing into the prevailing winds tends to be wetter than the side facing away. As air approaches the mountain range it is forced to rise and cool, condensing its water vapor and producing precipitation. Another climate maker is nearness to a body of water such as a large lake. Air flowing over the lake picks up moisture and deposits precipitation on areas downwind of the lake. For example, the area just east of the Great Lakes often receives large amounts of snow as the result of this "lake effect." Altitude is yet another factor. Temperatures fall about 6.5°C for every 1,000 meters of altitude above sea level. Finally, ocean currents can significantly alter weather patterns—making, for example, Great Britain and Scandinavia much warmer than expected for their latitudes. Wherever you live, the climate is the result of a number of such influences.

MATERIALS

- Pen or pencil
- Access to a world atlas and an encyclopedia
- Internet access

(continued)

Researching Climate and Climate Zones *(continued)*

 PROCEDURE

1. Choose one location each from List A, List B, and List C.

   List A: Singapore, Cairo (Egypt), Nairobi (Kenya)
   List B: Thule (Greenland), Nome (Alaska), Murmansk (Russia)
   List C: Buenos Aires (Argentina), Pyongyang (North Korea), Dijon (France)

2. From an atlas, encyclopedia, the Internet, and any other reference sources available to you, research the following climate facts for each chosen location and enter your results in Data Table 1. If necessary, convert units to match those shown in the table.

   • average temperature
   • average yearly precipitation

3. From your sources, research the following climate factors for each location and enter your results in Data Table 1.

   • altitude   • Distance to the nearest
   • latitude   large body of water

4. From the sources you used to gather information for steps 1, 2, and 3, or from other sources, find the same information for Pierre, South Dakota.

5. Compare the data you have gathered for each of the three locations with that for Pierre, South Dakota. Classify each area as tropical, temperate, or polar. (For reference, Pierre is a temperate, semiarid location.)

(continued)

Name _____ Date _____

 DATA COLLECTION AND ANALYSIS

Data Table 1

	Reference Location	Location 1	Location 2	Location 3
	Pierre			
average temperature °C	8.3			
average yearly precipitation cm	45			
altitude m	526			
latitude ±°	+44°			
distance to nearest water km (name of body of water)	1800 (Gulf of Mexico)			
classification	temperate, semiarid			

 CONCLUDING QUESTIONS

1. For each of the cities you have chosen, which of the three factors you researched (latitude, altitude, distance to nearest significant body of water) is the most influential in shaping the climate of that location? Which is the least influential?

_____

_____

_____

_____

(continued)

Researching Climate and Climate Zones *(continued)*

2. For the cities you have chosen, does any have a climate which cannot be explained by the three factors? Can you think of any additional factors that might help to explain the climate?

_____

_____

_____

_____

EXTENSION Repeat this exercise for the area where you live. Be sure to investigate possible climate makers that may affect your conclusion.

 FOLLOW-UP ACTIVITIES

1. Since other members of the class probably chose different cities to examine, compare your results with those of your classmates. Does this affect your conclusions about the predictability of climate based on the three climate factors you explored? Can you infer other climate factors that may be important in some locations?

2. Sometimes very local factors can create **microclimates**, which modify the climate in very small areas. These microclimates can affect human activity. For example, the moderating effect of the Finger Lakes in New York State makes it possible to grow grapes on their shores. Find a location in your area where the weather is generally different from the surrounding area. Research and write a brief report on what is different about the weather there and why.

The Greenhouse Effect

 ## INSTRUCTIONAL OBJECTIVES

Students will be able to

- demonstrate that heat can be trapped by an object, raising its temperature.
- recognize that different materials absorb different amounts of heat.
- explain how the greenhouse effect works in planetary atmospheres.

NATIONAL SCIENCE STANDARDS ADDRESSED

Students demonstrate an understanding of

- energy in the earth's system.
- changes in global climate.
- conservation of energy.
- transfer of energy.

Students demonstrate scientific inquiry and problem-solving skills by

- framing questions.
- using laboratory tools to measure phenomena.
- identifying and controlling variables in an experimental setting.

Students demonstrate effective scientific communication by

- arguing from evidence and data.
- representing data in multiple ways (follow-up activity).

MATERIALS

For each student:

- Thermometer readable to 0.5°F or 0.2°C
- Watch or clock
- Desk lamp with an incandescent bulb (not fluorescent)
- Bowl or cup, preferably white
- Clear, uncolored plastic food wrap
- Black paper or cloth (enough to cover the bottom of bowl)

HELPFUL HINTS AND DISCUSSION

Time frame: 50 minutes, or one class period
Structure: Individuals (at home) or pairs (in class)
Location: At home or in class

Be sure that each student has access to a lab-quality thermometer or digital electronic household thermometer. Students must know how to read a thermometer accurately and precisely. Be sure that they know what the divisions on the scale mean, and that they can read the thermometer to within 0.5°F or 0.2°C, estimating between divisions if necessary.

Diagram 1

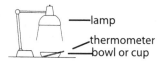

ADAPTATIONS FOR HIGH AND LOW ACHIEVERS

High Achievers: Encourage these students to do the Extension and Follow-up activities.

Low Achievers: Review the material prior to the experiment, particularly how to read a thermometer. Stress the need for careful experimental procedure, especially in timing the observations.

SCORING RUBRIC

Full credit should be given to students who answer all questions correctly and in complete sentences, and who complete the data table appropriately. Extra credit should be awarded to students who complete the Extention or Follow-up activities. The quiz can be scored from 1 to 4 correct.

 INTERNET TIE-INS   http://www.ed.uiuc.edu/COE/SNN/Jan-Feb.96/Greenhouse.html
http://www.covis.nwu.edu/Geosciences/projects/GLOBAL_WARMING/GE
/background1.html

 QUIZ   Fill in the correct word in each of the following.
1. The greenhouse effect makes our atmosphere _____ than it would be otherwise.
2. Carbon dioxide absorbs _____ radiation.
3. Without the greenhouse effect, Earth would be too _____ for life.
4. _____ is a place where the runaway greenhouse effect has created extremely hot conditions.

Name _____   Date _____

The Greenhouse Effect

 BEFORE YOU BEGIN

People are still debating whether burning fossil fuels and emitting wastes into the air are significantly changing Earth's atmosphere. It is important for everyone to understand that there may be risks due to these activities.

One potentially serious problem comes from what is called the **greenhouse effect.** In a greenhouse, energy from the sun is trapped and the temperature is raised, helping plants to grow. A planet's atmosphere can also act as a greenhouse. Here's how: The average surface temperature of Earth (or any planet) is determined by the balance between the energy it receives from the sun and the amount of energy it radiates out into space. Some of the sun's energy is absorbed by the surface, which re-emits it as infrared radiation. Most of this infrared radiation is released out into space. However, some of it is trapped by certain naturally-occurring gases in the atmosphere. This results in a higher temperature than there would be without those gases. This greenhouse effect warms Earth by about 30°C. Without it, Earth would be too cold for life to survive.

Through human activity, we are adding more gases to the atmosphere that are good at absorbing infrared radiation. Carbon dioxide is a major greenhouse gas. It comes from burning oil, natural gas, and coal as fuel, from clearing and burning forest land, and from plant and animal life. Other greenhouse gases include water vapor, methane, and Freon™, a refrigerant. Increased amounts of these gases will trap more infrared radiation, thus changing the balance between received and radiated energy. The result is the warming of the atmosphere and possible drastic changes in weather and climate. An extreme result could be a "runaway greenhouse effect" as on Venus (whose atmosphere is mostly carbon dioxide), where surface temperatures reach 500°C.

 ## MATERIALS

- Thermometer readable to as small a division as possible, at least 0.5°F or 0.2°C
- Watch or clock
- Desk lamp with an incandescent (not fluorescent) bulb
- Bowl or cup, preferably white
- Clear, uncolored plastic food wrap
- Black paper or cloth (enough to cover the bottom of bowl)

 ## PROCEDURE

1. Pick a shaded location away from sunlight. Set up a desk lamp so it points down onto a bowl as shown in Diagram 1. The bulb should be about 20–30 cm from the bottom of the bowl. Put a thermometer in the bowl. Be sure that the sensitive part of the thermometer is in the bottom of the bowl. Leave the lamp off.

2. To compare how much the temperature changes when the lamp is turned on, do the following: With the lamp still off, check the thermometer and record the temperature in Data Table 1. Convert to degrees Celsius if necessary, and record as precisely as possible. Now, turn the light on, wait three minutes, and record the temperature again in the Data Collection section. Turn the light off.

(continued)

The Greenhouse Effect *(continued)*

Diagram 1

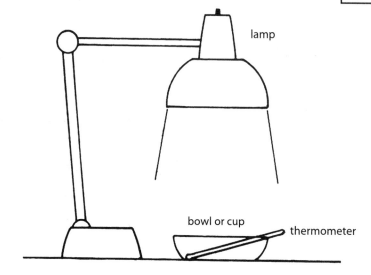

lamp

bowl or cup   thermometer

3. Wait at least three minutes with the light off. Cover the bowl tightly with clear plastic food wrap, keeping the sensitive part of the thermometer inside. Record the temperature. Turn the light on, wait three minutes, and record the temperature again in the Data Collection table. Turn off the light.

4. Remove the plastic wrap and thermometer. Again, wait at least three minutes with the light off. Line the bottom of the bowl with the black paper or cloth. Replace the thermometer and plastic wrap. Record the temperature. Turn the light on, wait three minutes, and record the temperature again. Turn off the light.

5. For each of steps 2, 3, and 4, calculate the change in temperature from "lamp off" to "lamp on." Record this difference in the Data Collection table.

EXTENSION Repeat this experiment several times using different lamps, different bowls or different materials in the bowl, and different clear covers. Try to keep the conditions of the experiment as uniform as possible. You will need to measure very carefully to see the resulting variations. Relate your results to the fact that not all greenhouse gases have an equal effect.

 DATA COLLECTION AND ANALYSIS

	Lamp off	Lamp on	Change
Bowl uncovered	_____ °C	_____ °C	_____ °C
Bowl covered with plastic wrap	_____ °C	_____ °C	_____ °C
Bowl lined with black and covered with plastic wrap	_____ °C	_____ °C	_____ °C

(continued)

The Greenhouse Effect (continued)

 CONCLUDING QUESTIONS

1. Did the temperature rise in step 2? Why? _____
   _____
   _____

2. Was the temperature rise in step 3 greater than, less than, or the same as that in step 2? Give a reason for this.
   _____
   _____

3. In which step did you get the greatest temperature rise?
   _____
   _____

4. Suppose that the situation in step 2 is a model of Earth without any atmosphere, and step 3 is similar to Earth with an atmosphere of natural composition. Step 4 is then comparable to what potential disaster condition?
   _____
   _____

⚡ FOLLOW-UP ACTIVITIES ⚡

Research the sources and amounts of the various greenhouse gases being emitted into the atmosphere, and write a report. Construct a pie chart showing the amounts of each of these gases in the atmosphere.

Share Your Bright Ideas with Us!

We want to hear from you! Your valuable comments and suggestions will help us meet your current and future classroom needs.

Your name_____Date_____

School name_____Phone_____

School address_____

Grade level taught_____Subject area(s) taught_____Average class size_____

Where did you purchase this publication?_____

Was your salesperson knowledgeable about this product?   Yes_____   No_____

What monies were used to purchase this product?

_____School supplemental budget   _____Federal/state funding   _____Personal

Please "grade" this Walch publication according to the following criteria:

Quality of service you received when purchasing ....A   B   C   D   F
Ease of use...A   B   C   D   F
Quality of content...A   B   C   D   F
Page layout ....A   B   C   D   F
Organization of material ....A   B   C   D   F
Suitability for grade level ....A   B   C   D   F
Instructional value..A   B   C   D   F

COMMENTS:_____

_____

What specific supplemental materials would help you meet your current—or future—instructional needs?

_____

Have you used other Walch publications? If so, which ones?_____

May we use your comments in upcoming communications?   _____Yes   _____No

Please **FAX** this completed form to **207-772-3105**, or mail it to:

Product Development, J. Weston Walch, Publisher, P.O. Box 658, Portland, ME 04104-0658

We will send you a **FREE GIFT** as our way of thanking you for your feedback.   **THANK YOU!**